T0149532

Fairies

Fairies

An Informative and Whimsical Guide

TONI KLEIN

FAIRIES
AN INFORMATIVE AND WHIMSICAL GUIDE

iUniverse books may be ordered through booksellers or by contacting:

iUniverse
1663 Liberty Drive
Bloomington, IN 47403
www.iuniverse.com
1-800-Authors (1-800-288-4677)

ISBN: 978-1-5320-5592-8 (sc)
ISBN: 978-1-5320-5593-5 (e)

Library of Congress Control Number: 2018909771

Print information available on the last page.

iUniverse rev. date: 09/11/2018

To my mother, Rowena, who believes that life should be lived with magic and wonder every single day.

To my grandmothers, Elizabeth and Nell, who, when I was a small child, introduced me to the fairy realm and to the magic that life may bring, if only you allow it.

Thank you for keeping the magic and mystery alive in my heart and mind.

CONTENTS

PREFACE

Hello! I'm Toni, author of *Passport to Heaven's Angelic Messages* (iUniverse 2016) and currently *Fairies*. I am a certified fairyologist and ACP—angel certified practitioner—at your service. In addition, I hold certifications in Reiki, past-life healing, and mediumship, and I'm trained in dream interpretation.

Fairies are a very interesting subject and are much more complex than we realize. When we hear the term *fairy*, I believe our minds immediately envision an endearing, tiny, mystical winged female, carrying a wand. She is our point of reference, but there is so much more!

My experience with the fairy realm came at a very young age. My book *Passport to Heaven's Angelic Messages* mentions that my communication with angels began as a little girl. When I first saw and felt evidence of the fairy, it was different from the angel, and I didn't understand it. However, the powerful females in my life—my mother and two grandmothers—made the difference clear to me.

My grandmothers could not have been more opposite, yet they both shared one thing in common; a belief in the fairy. One was of Irish descent from County Armagh, and the other was of pure German descent; her family has lived in this country for six generations. Each was of a different upstanding upbringing and lifestyle. My maternal grandmother was a sophisticated, free-spirited woman, married to an architect who worked in Manhattan during the Depression. My paternal grandmother was stern, hardworking, and highly fiscally independent. She and my grandfather bought and sold properties and farmed as a hobby. Still, they shared some commonalities. Both were personally successful and raised happy families, but the critical element they shared was the belief in the mystical fairy. Both experienced fairy sightings. My mother took after her mother psychically, and I followed both grandmothers into a true belief of the mystical world. Sadly, my grandmothers are both gone now, but I carry with me the excitement they imparted to me about the wonderful fairy.

My husband, John, often tells me that I am very much like the fairy. He states this due to the parallels in behavior they and I share—we adore glittery objects, sweets, and gifts, but the large component that draws us closely together is this: when I meet someone for the first time, I—similar to the fairy—have the knack of "scanning" the person's aura and instantly receive an unusually accurate vibe regarding his or her personality. I'm rarely fooled. John thinks it's uncanny. Because I possess this talent, he asks me to share my thoughts with him after meeting his business contacts.

The concept of the fairy is a multicultural and worldwide phenomenon. Most individuals are initially skeptical, wondering if the fairy is real. How can we claim it is not? Just because we cannot see it in human form doesn't negate the fact it lives alongside us.

The many inexplicable things in this world definitely make it a more interesting place to live. Some people take solace in the supernatural. Knowing there is more out there than meets the eye is exciting.

Whenever I broached the subject of the fairy, people would say a couple of similar statements without hesitation: "I really don't know what a fairy is," or "Is a fairy the same as an angel?" Then, seemingly interested, they immediately would follow up with the question, "How would I know if I saw a fairy?" Based on a poll and results I will share with you later, the participants claimed they didn't believe in the fairy. Hence, I felt compelled to share my knowledge on the subject. Plus, I have found it a duty and a pleasure to write this book for all who have an interest in fairy life.

Since experiencing, studying, and writing about the fairy and other elementals, I am aware there are certain fairy rules we should not tamper with: Do not litter, abuse the environment with pollutants or pesticides, or harm pets. Fairies are our angels of nature and are concerned with the well-being of the earth as a whole.

I am happy to have a belief in the unknown, and I'm sure many others subscribe to this philosophy. I have always said there is much more than what we can see with our eyes. As the late John Lennon once said, "I believe in everything until it's disproved. So I believe in fairies, the myths, dragons. It all exists, even if it's in your mind. Who's to say that dreams and nightmares aren't as real as the here and now?" Bless John Lennon. I agree with him and will continue to believe in those unseen things and the mysteries in life until disproven.

If this seems like a foreign concept to you, I wager you'll believe after you read *Fairies*. I have faith in the mystery behind the veil. I also believe in angels, miracles, and the wonders of this earth. There is so much that exists but cannot be seen. Yes, I *believe* in the fairy!

Enjoy your adventure!

INTRODUCTION

Welcome to the wonderful land of mystery and magic! Have you ever thought that fairies could be real? To most Americans, fairies are just a fantasy created for children's entertainment. However, my dear reader, I'm here to excitedly exclaim they are genuine and actually coexist with us. Their purpose on earth is to protect nature and the environment, guard us from dangerous pollution, and show love to our animal friends. Fairies do interact with people often because they care about human life. These "nature angels" serve as the guardians assigned by the Creator to watch over our wildlife, the environment, and us.

The idea for *Fairies* came to me as a message given by my angel team in conjunction with the fairies. I was prodded to write about this subject because they communicated that a great number of people today are unaware of their existence as well as their positive involvement in our world and for the human race. As a spiritualist, I wish to deliver the positive news that these beings bring forth goodness and light into our lives. They wish to remain unnoticed, however, as they contribute several benefits to humanity. Fairies have their own place and involvement on this earth.

The fairy family consists of different forms: pixies, elves, dwarfs, gnomes, goblins, sprites, and demons. This book will concentrate primarily on the pixie variety, yet I will explain the other varieties as well. Additional mystical beings such as elementals, unicorns, mermaids and even butterflies are added features to this book.

Overall, *Fairies* is both informative and enlightening, whimsical and breezy. In the first few chapters, you will gain education and insight into the differences between fairies and the elementals. Later chapters provide entertainment and include topics such as fairy-related party ideas, gardening concepts, crafting, delightful poetry, and much more. These fanciful chapters may bring out the child that resides in all of us. After all, the fairy's wish is fun for all!

A brief chapter-by-chapter overview follows:

Chapter 1—What Is a Fairy?

I provide an overview of the fabulous fairies, including tips on how to participate in their causes.

Chapter 2—Fairy Mannerisms

We will delve into the behavior of the fairy family. The life of the elf, dwarf, gnome, and leprechaun are detailed.

Chapter 3—Who Are the Elementals?

This chapter explains the meaning of the elemental realm. Also provided is an expansive list of the many legendary creatures who are said to walk this world with us, each carrying its own superstition and value to humankind.

Chapter 4—Signs of Being in the Midst of a Fairy

You will learn how to recognize and feel the presence of fairies, as well as how to make a connection with them.

Chapter 5—The Tooth Fairy

The origins surrounding this imaginary pixie are explained; plus, the dispute over the worth of a child's tooth is examined.

Chapter 6—Famous Fairies

This chapter offers an interesting look into a few noteworthy magical beings—for example, the Sugar Plum Fairy and fairy godmothers.

Chapter 7—Fairy Tale versus Folklore

This chapter clarifies the difference between fairy tale and folklore. Well-known fairy tales and assorted folktales are examined.

Chapter 8—Fairy Sightings

You'll read of truly thought-provoking cases featuring our mystical friends from the USA and around the world.

Chapter 9—Are You a Fairy Believer?

This chapter reviews the survey results from a random sampling I conducted. The difference between fairies and angels is also detailed.

Chapter 10—Fairy Entertainment and Amusement

This chapter offers whimsy and quaintness. Topics such as fairy entertaining, fairy outings, gardening methods, fairy foods, and craft ideas are introduced. These may serve as pleasurable family events, a child's amusement on a rainy afternoon, and so much more.

Chapter 11—My Personal Fanciful Poetry Collection

In this chapter, I offer my poetry, which is dedicated to the fairy as well as to the angelic realm. I've also added a few distinctive rhymes. You may use this poetry to enhance and personalize a greeting card or as a personal prayer or chant. Enjoy!

Chapter 12—Mystical-Inspired Identification

This chapter offers a glimpse at an imaginative sampling of mystical names. Babies, adored pets, and even vehicles may be personalized from this fanciful list.

Appendix 1—The Mysterious Unicorn and Mermaid
Appendix 2—The Spiritual Butterfly
Appendix 3—Magical True-Life Fairy Experiences

These three appendixes offer insight into nonfairy creatures that also add magic and splendor to our world. Appendixes 1 and 2 offer information on the enchanting unicorn, mermaid, and butterfly;

each carries its own story of beauty and illusion. Appendix 3 showcases real-life stories of those who have had contact with the magnificence of the fairy as well as the divine butterfly.

My desire is to entertain you while enriching your mind on the subject of fairies, folklore, and superstition. I'm confident that after you've read *Fairies*, you will have become an expert on the subject. Your family and friends will be amazed with your in-depth knowledge of the beings and may even enjoy a thoughtful, spiritual poetry note or the unforgettable fairy gathering that you host.

It was a true pleasure to pen *Fairies* for you.

Chapter 1

WHAT IS A FAIRY?

Let the little fairy in you fly!

—Rufus Wainwright

The fairy has been with us for thousands of years. A fairy, often referred to as a nature angel, is an immortal, supernatural being of nature who reside in gardens, woodlands, farms, and other natural settings. Fairies come in various sizes and shapes, ranging from nearly invisible to the naked eye to a few feet tall. While certain fairies are deemed beautiful, others are not. The fairy line has eight identifiable clans: demons, dwarfs, elves, gnomes, goblins, gremlins, pixies, and sprites.

Fairies can be found in virtually every culture in folklore and myths. Their appearance may differ between different civilizations but all refer to the fairy being. A fairy may also be referred to as fay, fae, realm of the fays, faerie, or faery.

The *Merriam-Webster* definition of a fairy is "a mythical being of folklore and romance usually having diminutive human form and magic powers."

The fairy originates from an alternate plane. Although they live side by side with us, their dimension exists at a slightly higher level than ours, called the ethereal plane. They have the power to move onto earth through portals, as they desire. One type called the flower fairy may take up residence in our gardens or plants or homes. Fairies reside all over the world. We don't need to travel a great distance or to Ireland to feel their presence. They are among us in the forests, wooded areas, and in nature overall. In spiritual circles, fairies are referred to as nature fairies, nature spirits, or guardians and were placed here to help us. They are under the supervision and guidance of the archangels.

The image of the fairy has morphed into many personalities over time, especially through the works of Walt Disney. Fairies possess a magical persona and their own dispositions and charm.

Fairy 101

Before a fairy will come near a human, the human must be open-minded and a believer; it is only then an individual may be able to sense the presence of a fairy. If the person is not a believer, a fairy can be in close proximity but will not bother with the human being. It seems believers are basically a product of the location in which they were raised and/ or by whom they were raised. For instance, Ireland, Australia, and Scotland all have a well-known belief and acceptance of the entity. My grandmother lived in Ireland and was a believer; I live in America, but I was raised on the belief.

Some folks warn us to never utter the word *fairy*. They claim it will infuriate the fairy, and the consequence will be the onset of a terrible headache. Please disregard this thinking, as it's an old wives' tale. If fairies are referred to with respect, it's acceptable to say the word. On the other hand, if your intention is to poke fun, my advice is not to utter the word at all. We humans appreciate being revered, as do fairies, and like humans, fairies have egos. This means that fairies have the ability to possess negative emotions, just as humans do, such as fear, anger, and jealousy. Fairies are caring beings who respect the earth. Their interest is in protecting the environment and animals. They are not pleased with humans who scatter litter, cause havoc such as starting forest fires, mistreat animals, use toxic chemicals or speak ill of fairies. When we live kind, respectful lives, as we all should, the fairies will come forth and assist us in our earthly plights. As with the heavenly angels, we must request the assistance of the fairy. They may aid us with our finances or careers or offer guidance with children or the environment. Fairies do expect a favor each time they aid us, such as our picking up trash or another kind gesture dedicated to their earthly causes. Angels, however, would appreciate a kind deed demonstrated, yet no strings are attached.

In the event you are interested in partnering with the fairy and its causes, feel free to follow my seven-point guidelines:

1. Believe! Believe! Open your heart and mind to the possibility. Without faith, it's a lost cause.
2. Love your fellow man, animals, plant life, and all other living things.
3. Care for the environment by not using chemicals and by collecting litter and placing it in its proper receptacle. Care for animals, flowers, and plants. For example, volunteer at an animal shelter, a fund-raising project, or a town trash-collection project. (Be sure to use eco-friendly bags.) If your schedule doesn't allow the time to volunteer, don't fret! All of us can avoid littering, be kind to pets, and pick up a wrapper if we see it.
4. Be a person filled with goodness and gratitude. Enjoy life. Dance and play often. This positivity will be mirrored right back to you.
5. Speak to these beings silently or aloud. Fairies adore communication from those with pure hearts. Hold mental discussions with the fairies. They are listening. Fairies love to aid farmers with crops, assist with a garden, tend to children's dilemmas—they love children—and help with finances. Once the request is made, watch for signs—you surely will receive them.

6. Feel free to ask for comfort or support, as need, but remember it's imperative to give back in some way. This might be visiting the sick, adopting orphaned animals, feeding the hungry, or contributing to a clothing drive.

7. The fairies love gifts. Fairies love sparkly items. Examples are glistening crystals, polished rocks, wrapped sweet treats, or even playing music dedicated to them. If you play an instrument, offer a sweet melody—that is certainly a good way to give back. It is also a nice idea to reward them by displaying good behavior toward others. Naturally, candy is on their favorites list. Placing an unwrapped piece of candy in the garden is cause for a fairy celebration. Basically, you will receive what you give. Fairies are willing to help you, but it isn't a one-way street.

Fairies are members of our earthly society. Although they cannot be seen by the human eye unless they wish it, fairies are definitely among us.

Faeries, come take me out of this dull world,
For I would ride with you upon the wind,
Run on the top of the dishevelled tide,
And dance upon the mountains like a flame.

—William Butler Yeats
"The Land of Heart's Desire," 1894

Chapter 2

FAIRY MANNERISMS

The Fairies are invisible and inaudible like angels.
But their magic sparkles in nature.

—Lynn Holland

Fairies have their own distinct personalities. They have likes and dislikes, special places to live, and a fascinating existence. I have been questioned at times about the life of the fairy. What are fairies like? Where do they live? How do they dress? Do they speak? What about nicknames?

As mentioned, fairies have egos similar to those of humans. This relates to their feelings of self-worth, so negative emotions may arise such as jealousy, possessiveness, and vindictiveness. Yet similar to us mortals, fairies also demonstrate a loving, caring side for those who show respect to them, the environment, animals, and each other. In the past, fairies were deemed as frightening, but because the spiritual society has brought forth positive news of late, these misunderstood creatures are getting the positive press they deserve.

The Personality of the Elemental Fairies

The characteristics of the fairy are vast but stay within a central theme. The following list offers those characteristics in a fast and easy format, as fairies prefer their style of living.

- Is playful, fun-loving
- Is highly intelligent
- Is carefree; lives in the moment
- Has no fear of punishment
- Impulsive, frisky
- Is whimsical
- Has his or her own motives
- Loves to party; enjoys fairy gatherings, especially during a full moon
- Enjoys music (Beloved instruments are the harp, fiddle, tambourine, drums, cymbals, and whistles.)
- Is shy; does not like to be seen by humans
- Desires to live invisibly
- Appears and disappears, as desired
- Is private; reserved
- Keeps a secret very well
- Places a high value in neatness
- May transform to avoid being seen or captured
- Is supernatural, immortal, magical
- Is empowered with the ability to stretch or shorten time at will
- Is quirky; odd
- Is mischievous; a prankster
- May be kind or may be not so nice
- Is emotional; experiences feelings strongly; easily offended\
- May reward a human with good fortune, if deserving
- Appreciates humans who are good to the earth and animals
- Is helpful and generous, especially in the household and with farmers
- Is thoughtful; assists the needy by leaving helpful items

- May pull tricks on humans who are mean
- Has the power to place a spell on a human

Also of note:

- Town dwellers claim that a female fairy has the power to capture a man by hypnotizing him if she so desires.
- Fairy time does not match the human clock. A century lived by a human being may only be twenty-four hours to the fairy.

Fairy Disapproval

Fairies frown upon certain behavior. They do not care to be spied on or to have their playtime disrupted. Since they live in nature, the environment is highly revered. One goal of the fairy is to guard the earth, ensuring it is not destroyed in any way. If the earth is threatened, in that moment the fairy will flex his or her wings. For instance, if a fairy witnesses a human littering or torturing an animal, that person may sense sudden, agonizing head pain. In some cases, if negative behavior occurs, a quick storm or blizzard may take palce. Fairies abhor violence and brutal behavior.

What do fairies eat? Where do they live? How do they dress? Each fairy family (dwarfs, elves, gnomes, or leprechauns) has its own style of living, including certain food preferences, style of dress, and favored locale of residence.

Appearance and Size

The fairy families vary in size from minuscule to four feet tall to human-sized or larger.

The diminutive flying fairy closely resembles a human, yet there are differences. They have large eyes, pointy ears, and insect-like wings. This well-known fairy is very tiny and reaches a maximum of only five inches in height. We often refer to this type as the well-known Tinker Bell.

Dwarfs, also called Stout Folk because of their stocky builds, may weigh as much as a human male, but are very small in stature, standing at most only a few feet tall. Most are bald with hazel eyes. Female dwarfs are slightly thinner and taller. They are very polite, hold vast wisdom, and are loyal.

Dwarfs are powerful, wise magical beings who live in the mountains and mine for coal. They work at night and do not wish to be seen during daylight hours. If this occurs, the dwarf may permanently turn to stone.

You may remember seeing Disney's *Snow White and the Seven Dwarfs* at some point in your life. The evil queen wants to kill Snow White, so Snow White flees into the woods, where she meets seven dwarfs. They are thrilled to have her company, as she cleans and keeps their house while they mine for jewels. I'd say that was not a bad deal for the dwarfs.

Elves may grow up to seven feet tall. The elf looks like a little old man with pointed ears, a tiny body, long hair, and luminous skin. Women elves, on the other hand, are young and beautiful. Both genders are empowered with supernatural gifts, so the elf may choose to help or hinder at will. Folklore says that if an adult, child, or horse awakens with a terrible hair knot, it was the prank of an elf. This condition is known as "elf locks." Most likely the elf was exerting his or her power to punish those who do not behave admirably.

The gnome is a small, stubby character with a potato-like head. Gnomes may be a few inches tall to as tall as three feet. They wear bright pointed hats and solid-colored clothes, and they love to sport a big, bushy white beard. Gnomes are the garden keepers. Many people place statues of gnomes in their yards or gardens.

The leprechaun is a male being who adores his elaborate green suit, fancy hat, and shoes. He has red hair and stands approximately three feet tall. A cobbler by trade, his shoes are the very best in the land. He knows exactly where the pot of gold is located. Humans hope the leprechaun will lead them to it, but they can never catch him because he is so fast moving.

Remember the advertising slogan, "Lucky Charms—they're magically delicious"? This was said by both the leprechaun and children in the commercial that advertised Lucky Charms breakfast cereal, manufactured by General Mills. This delicious breakfast treat was made of oats and marshmallows and fashioned into different shapes. In the commercial, Lucky the leprechaun is forever being chased by kids who want his Lucky Charms cereal. The image of Lucky is perfection—an elusive, small man with red hair and a green hat and coat. As I was writing this, I heard of the passing of Arthur Anderson, who was the original voice of Lucky the leprechaun, at age ninety-three. May he find all the happiness and magic in the afterlife that he spread to all of us here on earth. As a child, I ate Lucky Charms. I loved digging out the marshmallows and eating those, leaving a box of oat cereal behind.

Fairy Food Preferences

In general, fairies are attracted to dairy foods—milk, cream, butter—bread, honey, mushrooms, and nuts. They also enjoy receiving a fun treat left by us humans. Hard candies, chocolate, and fruit are super gifts. Once the household retires for the evening, fairies may just help themselves. If you awake and things are missing, it may be your resident fairy at play!

Each type in the fairy group has its own special food choices. Dwarfs tend to enjoy meat. Interestingly, they are resilient to all poisons and will never suffer from food bacteria. Elves and leprechauns both delight in nuts, potatoes, and mushrooms and drink dandelion tea. The gnome group enjoys consuming roots and herbs.

Do Fairies Speak?

Yes, fairies speak, but it isn't like the human voice. The voice of the diminutive fairy is very squeaky. A human may hear them only if the fairies wish it. Again, the human must be open, receptive, and sincere in order to capture the fairy message. Elves, dwarfs, and gnomes have deeper, more manlike voices, while leprechauns love to sing.

The Fairy Residence

The fairy clans are among us in various locations—on the ground level, beneath the earth, under rocks, inside trees, in the forest, among the woods, and in gardens. They gravitate toward unpopulated areas, as privacy is a huge concern to them. Fairies like to keep their eyes on us, yet at the same time, they desire to remain unseen. Although fairies exist on Earth, they do travel back and forth between dimensions often and easily.

Fairies are considered solitary and live alone, or they engage in *trooping*, meaning they travel together in groups. All prefer to exist in natural settings, especially since the environment is their key interest. Correspondingly, nature keeps their energy charged and balanced.

Humans occupy houses, apartments, condos, and even houseboats, while fairies reside in fairy forts (better known as mounds or *raths*), caves, or trees or under rocks. Depending on the elemental and its lifestyle, housing may vary accordingly. Some live in the trunks of trees, in mountains or valleys, or hidden in mysterious mini-houses. For instance, a household brownie would most likely fit the kitchen personality and choose to live behind a kitchen hearth. Other sorts may gravitate toward unpopulated areas and may live in deep oceans, caves, and streams.

Fairy Dwellings

Dwarfs tend to dwell in caves and mountains. They populate the central region of the earth's continents.

Elves sit on a shelf during the holidays to make sure children behave—I'm joking! Elves are very popular in Iceland and take up residence beneath very large rocks. The wood elves live in trees. In the North Pole region, elves prefer to locate in kingdoms, forests meadows, or hollowed-out trees.

Gnomes gravitate toward gardens and forests and near ponds. These creatures have the ability to move through the earth as easily as we humans walk upon it. Gnomes are the guardians of secret underground treasures.

Leprechauns are thought to be found only in Ireland, but I assure you, they also exist in other enchanted regions. Leprechauns are hard to pin down and always on the run because they feel humans are always after their precious pot of gold.

How Does the Fairy Dress?

The style of dress depends upon the fairy. Each grouping has different tastes. Some fairies love to be in full fancy dress. Favorite fairy colors are green and red.

Do Other Names for the Fairy Exist?

The people who dwelled in the villages of yesteryear were frightened to call this being a fairy. It was believed it might offend the being or bring villagers bad luck. Instead, they chose to replace the nam *fairy* with other names. That way, no ill luck would be sent their way, and it also was a form of endearment. The following are a few of the charming tags given as a form of respect and to stand in the good graces of the fairy:

- Good folk
- Wee people
- Fair folk
- Hidden people

- People of the mounds
- Little people

In short, fairies love pleasure, beauty, and splendor; grace of movement; music; and everything artistic. They do not like any sort of violent behavior or brutal enjoyment. They hate greedy people who gather the last bit of grain, drain the last bit of milk from the glass, or pluck the trees bare of fruit, leaving nothing for the spirits who wander past in the moonlight.

If treated well, the fairies will bestow good fortune and reveal the mysteries of plant herbs. For acts of kindness bestowed upon the spirits, fairy blessings will come in the form of unexpected good luck.

The fairies are a very distinct group of beings. Like humans, they have their own traits, passions, likes, dislikes, motivations, and egos. Generally, fairies are kind, well-meaning beings who try to exist in this world, just as we do. Similar to us, fairies may become offended or elated by another's treatment. If treated kindly, they may bestow good fortune, yet if they are hurt, they can act mischievously. Therefore, always be on good behavior, and be kind to strangers—he or she may be a fairy prince or princess in disguise who has come to test your kindness and virtue.

Tink was not all bad: or, rather, she was all bad just now, but, on the other hand, sometimes she was all good. Fairies have to be one thing or the other, because being so small they unfortunately have room for one feeling only at a time. They are, however, allowed to change, only it must be a complete change.

—J. M. Barrie, *Peter Pan*

Chapter 3

WHO ARE THE ELEMENTALS?

Faeries, come take me out of this dull world,
For I would ride with you upon the wind,
Run on the top of the dishevelled tide,
And dance upon the mountains like a flame.

—William Butler Yeats
"The Land of Heart's Desire," 1894

The elementals comprise a large list of magical beings. The fairy realm is only a portion of the elemental class. What is an elemental? According to the website Urban Dictionary, "An elemental is a mythical creature which is related to a specific element of matter (fire, earth, wind, water), usually they have humanlike qualities such as limbs; in some cases, they have a face."

Each category of elementals has a different purpose. The elemental realm resides here on earth and also on the ethereal plane. The ethereal plane is a separate plane located right above earth. The elementals have the ability to share the planet with us on our earthly level, on the subterranean level, and in the air. At will, an elemental has the ability to dart back and forth between planes as desired.

Interest in the elemental realm was high during the Middle Ages and the Renaissance. Paracelsus, who lived during the sixteenth century, formulated serious discussions and documented his theories regarding the elementals. Paracelsus was an acclaimed Swiss German physician, as well as an alchemist, a healer, and an astrologer. He formulated an astounding connection between Aristotle's four elements (earth, air, wind, and fire) and living beings. He paired these groupings and then assigned names to each.

- Gnomes—earth
- Undines—water
- Sylphs—air
- Salamanders—fire

Paracelsus professed that God created the elementals in order to protect their corresponding elements. For example, Undines watched over our bodies of water (streams, lakes, oceans). Air people, the sylphs, assisted with the air quality and regulated storms. Gnomes regulated the earth, while Salamanders regulated fire.

Paracelsus envisioned the elementals as smaller humans who engaged in both good and bad personality traits and were a bit crafty and rather amusing. He thought their mannerisms were comparable to those of the human being, but they differed because they possessed supernatural powers.

In my opinion, Paracelsus was a forward thinker. He was born in 1493 and practiced medicine in the 1500s. Paracelsus was the father of toxicology. He felt that a doctor should have knowledge of chemistry in order to effectively treat the patient. He knew that certain agents could be poisonous in great amounts, yet prescriptions given in smaller accurate amounts could actually cure the patient. Paracelsus was the first to profess that an illness was related to the setting in which a person lived or was employed. He drew a parallel between a miner's physical symptoms and his work environment. He claimed that mines posed a serious health risk to the miners. Paracelsus was instrumental in the strides made in medicine today. Plus, his belief in supernatural forces and the elementals was inspiring. Back in the sixteenth century, he walked on very dangerous territory by claiming such entities did exist. I am grateful, centuries later, that we have gained insight from Paracelsus's studies and theories.

It wasn't long before talk of the elementals and their existence by Paracelsus and other like-minded individuals was silenced by religious figures of the organized churches. Certain leaders overrode popular thought, as they sought conformity and claimed that elementals were false or evil. Today, society is much more accepting and holds diverse thoughts and beliefs. In the modern world, the value of the elemental is acknowledged, as is the realization that they pose no threat to one's religious beliefs or the church.

The elementals are fun-loving but may be perceived as dangerous, as they may—as a form of play—create a sudden thunderstorm or blizzard. All play is not so bold or random, though. They do have the humans' best interests at heart and do wish to coexist on the planet with us.

The supernatural spirits of the elements come in many different shapes and sizes, and their living quarters vary, depending upon their type. Let's explore the different forms and their habitats.

Earth Elementals

The major earth elemental is known as the gnome. Others do exist, but gnomes are the elemental that Paracelsus assigned to the earth. Fairies, pixies, elves, wood nymphs, and brownies fall into the earth elemental category. Green is the color most associated with the earthly group. As discussed, fairies come in an array of sizes from a few inches in height to a few feet tall. Some have wings and are able to fly, while others are only able to walk.

Brownies

Brownies are known as the household elves, and they possess guardian tendencies. Brownies are tiny men who may choose to take up residence in a household. While the family is sleeping, brownies are very happy to conduct odd jobs and other chores for the family. (Wow, I love that!) In return for their toil, they would appreciate a bowl of cream. If not rewarded properly, brownies could cause havoc by smashing plates or other kitchen items. If the family is lucky, the brownie may just vacate and move in with a more appreciative family. Just remember if you wake up and your kitchen chores have been completed, and you have no knowledge of they were done, chalk it up to a brownie. Yours is a lucky household. Don't forget to leave the cream!

Brownies are approximately three feet tall, dress in brown clothing, and have brownish skin and shaggy hairstyles. Most likely, they will remain incognito.

Pixies

Pixies are very pretty and tiny beings. They appear childlike, have pointy ears, and dress in green. Pixies love to play and are known to express jealousy. Tinker Bell is a pixie.

Devas

The deva supervises the lower order of fairies, such as the tree or flower fairy. Devas appear radiant, are very intelligent, and understand the workings of the universe. This is easy for devas, as they have an association with its law and order. Today's very popular term *diva* is not the same as the elemental deva. The word diva may be used to refer to a very gifted female singer or as slang for a self-centered, prima donna female.

Elves

Elves are friendly and happy spirits who enjoy music, dance, and celebration. Elves are a race that forms their own civilizations, similar to human communities. Elves locate themselves way under the earth's surface but also may reside inside trees. They are hard workers and mild-mannered. If threatened, however, elves may choose to use magical powers to cast a spell on the human who upsets them. If elves let their guard down, they may be spotted by human beings. They are the easiest to see yet may disappear in an instant if they choose. Elves are secretive, guard their property, and love rainfall. They can hear the thoughts of our hearts. If we ask for assistance, and an elf hears our mental wish, he will grant it. Elves are well-meaning and do not like discontent in the world.

As a country, Iceland strongly believes in the reality of elves. Iceland road-planning organizations take elf residences into consideration when building a new road or bypass. They want to ensure that any new construction does not disrupt a place that is believed to be an elf dwelling. If it does, the road will be redirected around the elves' home area, not through it. I heard a story of a massive rock that was located at the top of hill in a small town in Iceland. One day a man who wished to build his house where the boulder was located asked the builders to remove it. After a few tries, it was determined that the rock was impossible to break and relocate. A native to the area urged the buyer to beware and not to build there, as an elf family most likely lived under the rock. He further cautioned the buyer that if he continued, the builder would be sorry and endure hardships. Fortunately, the man was wise, took heed, and moved to another site. Many people state emphatically not to tamper with the residence of an elf or to beware of the consequences.

> *Keebler elves*: A very popular depiction of elves are the Keebler elves. As a child, I loved the clever animated commercials made by the Keebler company, in which a very endearing elf named Ernie Keebler oversees a group of elves named the Keebler elves. They make and bake a variety of snacks in a factory, which is located

inside a hollow tree. Their factory as well as their residence is in the same tree. That is the perfect depiction of the elf's style of living. The Keebler elves are portrayed as a very hardworking bunch, which is a true characteristic of the elf. In my opinion, the commercials are genius. Kudos to Keebler founder, Godfrey Keebler; Kellogg's (the parent company); and the advertising agency that developed this fun and accurate depiction, while bringing the elf to the forefront of the public eye.

Santa's elves: These elves, also known as "Christmas elves," were made popular through literature in the late 1800s and are now an important holiday staple for those who reside in the United States, Ireland, and Canada, just to name a few countries. These tiny people assist Santa Claus and live with him at the North Pole. Their prime concern is to work in Santa's workshop, crafting toys for children and tending to the reindeer. These elves have made my son, Ian, very happy on numerous Christmases.

Gnomes

Gnomes live underground, while the fairies live on the earth's surface in gardens, trees, woods, and forests. According to an article on the website Luna's Grimoire (2012), "The Fae and Elementals: The Realm of Earth," Paracelsus stated,

> The type of gnome most frequently seen is the brownie, or elf, a mischievous and grotesque little creature from twelve to eighteen inches high, usually dressed in green or russet brown. Most of them appear as very aged, like old men, often with long white beards, and their figures are inclined to rotundity. They can be seen scampering out of holes in the stumps of trees and sometimes they vanish by actually dissolving into the tree itself.

In the event a gnome comes in contact with a human, the gnome will shape-shift into human form. He will appear as a stocky, short, older, small humanlike being. Gnomes may aid us humans in attracting money and fulfill our material needs if they feel we honestly need it. If they are near us, hear our plea, and deem us worthy, they will send help to us. The major job and concern of the gnome while living on the earth plane is our planet's vital energy resource. They serve as anchors of the earth's magnetic energy field and direct it properly. In addition, they trigger energy lines and maintain these lines around the world. All energy hubs in the land are a concern to gnomes because they want them to function properly. In fact, any sacred sites that are built on energy hot spots are especially guarded by the gnomes.

Gnome Fun Facts

- Gnomes construct their households beneath very mature trees and take good care of the undergrowth.
- Gnomes prefer to go out in the evening only. They are especially animated at this time of day.
- Gnomes are animal advocates. They are able to communicate in the same language with them and generally safeguard our wildlife population. It is not uncommon for fowl, such as pheasants, to have a gnome as a spiritual guardian.
- Gnomes gravitate toward energy centers. They have the power to ramp up the energy lines in order to make them more powerful, as they feel appropriate.
- Gnomes wear pointy hats and have large noses.
- Gnomes are very wise because they have access to several of the earth's mysteries. If a gnome chooses to communicate with a human being, much wisdom will be imparted.

It is extremely beneficial for the human race to sincerely believe in and befriend gnomes.

Water Elementals

The water elemental is the undine or the water fairy. Paracelsus created the term in the sixteenth century. Undines resemble humans and are graceful, smart, and cunning and their bodies shimmer. Others who fall into the water elemental group include mermaids, mermen, nymphs, water goblins, and sprites. Undines reside in all water avenues—ocean caves, the sea, fresh water, brooks, rivers, waterfalls, fountains, lakes, marshes and clouds that are filled with moisture. An individual may experience the presence of a water elemental if a sudden, cold burst of air is felt while sitting near a spring.

The water spirits manage chemistry. For instance, they may form an attraction between two people, help rekindle love, or heal a person from an amorous upset. Moreover, they can help us develop our psychic senses. If they choose to present themselves, we might see a flash of color before us or actually witness a mermaid. Undines are interested in the flow of water and how it corresponds to human emotions, as the full moon and ocean tides are said to have an effect on us. They are friendly and inviting but cannot normally be seen with the naked eye unless they approve it.

The subgroups of the water undines consist of mermaids, sea maids (a goddess of the sea), potamides (sea snails), naiads, oceanids, and oreads (nymphs).

Air Elementals

According to Paracelsus, the sylph is an air elemental, although there are other varieties. Sylphs are the keepers of the wind and are seen as feminine energy with magical abilities. Sylphs glide through the air and do not live anywhere except in the wind. Their mission is to purify the air. Today, sylphs have their work cut out for them since pollution seems greater than ever. In addition to pollution control, sylphs exert authority over cloud formation, rainfall, monsoons, droughts, and regulating weather conditions overall.

Air Fairies

The air fairy is similar to the traditional children's book fairies—sweet and fanciful. Their interest is in guiding us in our spiritual advancement as well as maintaining the balance of the earth and skies. Air fairies reside in very high altitudes and therefore may act as mediators of the wind and storms. These fairies assist our planet by controlling the winds, helping in the migration of birds, and even assisting those who travel on planes. Take notice when an air elemental is near. Each time you notice a tiny tornadolike gust of dirt or leaves, an air fairy is at play!

Have you ever awakened with a sandlike sensation in the corner of your eye? When I was young, my mother told me an air fairy had come into my room and tossed magic dust into my eyes while I was sleeping. She was able to turn an irritating eye sensation into a situation that made me feel like a million bucks! This is another example of the playfulness of the air fairy.

Fire Elementals

Paracelsus linked the salamander to the element of fire. Fire elementals denote protective energy, the creation of new things, and the devastation of what no longer needs to exist. They represent passion, quick impulses, and courage, such as is seen in the rebellious behavior of a teenager.

Legend has it that the salamander was born of fire. Campers have mentioned to me that they have witnessed the genesis of a salamander in the spark of the campfire. Salamanders are considered the most powerful of all of the elementals and tend to lend a spiritual helping hand to those in distress.

What Are Other Examples of Elementals?

Brief descriptions of the mystical personalities of other types of elementals follow for your reading pleasure. Later, you may wish to dazzle your friends or be the fun personality at the party with your newfound knowledge.

Banshee

The banshee is an Irish female fairy known for her loud wailing noises. Unfortunately, her crying is said to forecast an impending death. She produces squealing sounds when she communicates bad news. The banshee's appearance is often unsettling, yet she has the ability to convert herself into a beautiful woman at will. She is often seen wearing green clothing.

Bogeyman

The bogeyman is male figure. Parents inform their children that he exists in order to terrify them and to gain control and obedience. It is said that the bogeyman will appear to youngsters only in the dark, and he usually hides in the closet. He waits for these scared children to drift off to sleep before he pops out. Scary, huh? My advice is this: Just behave.

Over the years, films have depicted the bogeyman in many ways. The 1934 film *Toyland*, starring Laurel and Hardy, featured the bogeyman. In the movie, Bogeyland is located across from Toyland, with an alligator-filled body of water separating the two worlds. Do not commit a crime in Toyland, for those who do will be shipped to Bogeyland for punishment, never to return again. Frightening! That's Hollywood, and we love it!

Let's fast-forward in time to films of the recent past. The *Halloween* series of movies features Michael Myers, the boy who is termed "the bogeyman." We think in each movie he has finally been killed. Yet as Tommy tells his sister, Laurie, in the original 1978 *Halloween* film, "You can't kill the bogeyman."

Changeling

A changeling is a fairy who swaps its own baby and for a human one. This is done in secret, and the human parent is oblivious to the switch.

Some storytellers claim the human children live happily in their new fairyland home, while the fairy baby living in the human family does not quite fit in. The good news is that in some cases, the fairy will return the human baby to its real parents. Why do they take the baby in the first place? Because they can.

Flower Fairies

These particular fairies are young and pretty and sport insectlike wings. They have a passion for dancing and frolicking about gardens. They guard and communicate with the flowers.

Goblins

A goblin's main concern is seeking and attaining the treasures of the earth. They are considerate of the planet and live beneath the ground. Goblins are kind to those who have exhibited kindness to them. Goblins are rather scary-looking with bulging eyes. They reside in caves and are secretive beings. Goblins are considered the outlaws of the fairy group.

Monaciello

The people of Naples, Italy, believe in a monklike fairy. The monaciello is described as a tiny man who disguises himself under a robe and hood similar to the clothing worn by a monk. He resides in the vicinity of a monastery and travels through secret passageways. Italian folklore declares that the monaciello fairy is interested in helping the poor by appearing to needy humans in a dark alley. If they are so bold as to follow the fairy, they will benefit monetarily because the fairy monk is leading them to hidden treasure. Kindly, no payback is expected, but this fairy loves to play tricks as well. If you ever are in Naples or the surrounding area, be aware that blankets or articles of clothing may be pulled off your body. This may be the fairy acting as a trickster.

Tree Spirits

Numerous cultures are familiar with the tree fairies. Typically, these are female goddess entities who protect tree life. Celtic traditions believe trees have nature spirits and are blessed. Trees that offer medicinal benefits are considered the most sacred. Ancient Egyptians believed in the existence of a lady of the sycamore, the Egyptian goddess Hathor. Her tree is a sycamore fig tree, however, not the sycamore tree that grows in the United States. The juice of the fruit on this tree offers medicinal benefits. Hathor is an excellent example of a tree fairy.

Trolls

Trolls are popular beings in Scandinavian legend. For the most part, trolls are considered to be male. They may be very small or humongous, but either way, they are hideous-looking creatures. Trolls dwell under inaccessible rocks or in caves. They do not settle in alone but in family units. Trolls do not care about helping humankind.

When I was a child, troll dolls were the rage. These dolls were a few inches tall and had cute, brightly colored hair that was frizzy and wild. Today, the troll dolls are popular again due to the new animated film *Trolls* (2016) by DreamWorks. It stars Justin Timberlake and Anna Kendrick and focuses on trolls who aspire to protect their troll settlement from being alienated. The Hollywood-version trolls are appealing, colorful, and endearing in appearance and voice.

Water Babies

Water fairies naturally live near the seashore. They do not reside deep in the ocean but hang out on the outskirts. These creatures are happy and fun-loving. Water babies are slender, care about sea life, and help maintain harmony and order in the sea.

Will-o'-Wisps

Will-o'-wisps are naughty fairies who have the reputation for bad behavior. They secretly take away the lanterns of unsuspecting, fatigued travelers and shine them into the distance. Sojourners will then follow this light in hope of finding the way to their destinations. This glowing orb, however, retreats farther and farther away into nothingness. This foolery eventually places voyagers into perilous situations.

Snow Fairies

These enchanting beings are the caretakers of the snow. As snow falls, it is purified with spiritual energy. Snow fairies deliver a sense of calm to the land with every snowfall. I always find it a quiet and serene time after each fresh snowfall, and I know it is the work of the snow fairies.

The elementals work hard to keep the world balanced for all humankind. Certainly, a sense of peace and renewal may be felt when we're near the water or are outdoors or in nature. Elementals assist humankind but wish to remain invisible and anonymous. Elementals possess special powers and congregate in trees, gardens, and other natural settings. They are not attracted to the hustle and bustle of city living and generally stay away, choosing country living.

The energy of the city is noticeably different from that of rural life. We must remember to be respectful of elementals and their way of life. It is truly amazing that so many varieties coexist with us on earth. We all have a job to do here, and elementals are no exception.

Did you ever hear
Of the frolic fairies dear?
They're a blessed little race,

Peeping up in fancy's face,
In the valley, on the hill,
By the fountain and the rill;
Laughing out between the leaves
That the loving summer weaves.

—Frances Sargent Osgood

Chapter 4

SIGNS OF BEING IN THE MIDST OF A FAIRY

"David tells me that fairies never say 'We feel
happy'; what they say is, 'We feel dancey.'"

—J. M. Barrie, *Peter Pan in Kensington Gardens*

Is it possible to see or feel the presence of a fairy? Yes, of course it is. In order to be receptive, just like an antenna, the golden rule is to be open-minded and welcoming. Fairies are waiting for the right people with the right minds and intentions to find them. They are waiting for someone like you! Once this is apparent, everything will flow and become second nature—but it's up to you.

Fairies are closer than you think. They are all around us and are found on every continent in the world. It's all in the mind-set of the individual as to whether the fairy will come forward. As well as being receptive and open-minded, it's also important to be spiritually connected to Mother Earth to experience fairy life. A skeptic, nonbeliever, or person with ill intentions will never be able to see the fairy kingdom. In addition, those who do not care for the well-being of the earth or those who are staunch religious types who would never entertain the idea of fairies will not be likely candidates to see or feel the presence of fairies. That's not to say that the fairies wouldn't have a bit of fun by playing mischievous tricks on that sort of individual, but fairies only show themselves to people who are true of heart and pure of soul.

My Irish grandmother was a wealth of information on the subject of fairies. When she spoke, I listened intently—I was a sponge. A few of the many things she shared was that fairies love music, especially the flute. If music is played softly, especially live flute music, they will come close. If you play it in the quiet calmness of the woods, perhaps while you are camping or on a special fairy excursion, you may hear the rustling of leaves or the ringing of bells nearby. Pond ripples in a quiet body of water, when no evidence of life is around, is another fairy sign.

When seeking fairy activity, be aware of five telltale signs: (1) movement, (2) sight, (3) sound, (4) sensation, and (5) random fairy communication.

1. Movement
Fairies are very quick-moving beings. They flutter and dart about rapidly and are not known to fly in a straight line. Their movement is compared to a haphazard type of flying. People have commented that they have detected a flickering or a flash of sudden light from the corner of their eyes, which is a sign of the fairy's presence.

2. Sight
The way to see fairies is by the light they emit. Fairies are composed of energy; therefore, they radiate light. They are very playful, bouncy, and spirited presences, and they dance and spring about. Their light is so colorful that it may be described as a party lights. If you notice a twinkling, sparkly light nearby, don't be nervous. It's a sign the fairies are present!

When this first happened to me when I was younger, I thought my eyes were really tired or playing tricks. Then, I remembered my grandmother's recollection of a similar incident in Ireland. Furthermore, if privileged, you may even witness a vaporous form (not quite solid, as is a human form) or an orb of light buzzing quickly around in a circle.

Fairies are attracted to the hills. Native Americans are well aware of this and have encountered them. If you wish to see a fairy and enjoy the quiet and solitude of the mountains, fairies can be found there. Native Americans claim if they knock on tree wood, immediately leave a gift by the tree, and then hide, a fairy will come to claim the gift. Also, legend has it, that if a fairy believer gazes through a stone with a hole in it, a fairy may be seen.

Recently, a few acquaintances of mine decided to plan a fairy expedition into the woods in the hope of seeing a fairy or two. They were aware that fairies are attracted to water and can be found just by a person's sitting near a peaceful body of water. The planning was well thought; for optimum results, they chose a serene area and waited for good weather conditions and until they had the proper amount of time so they wouldn't feel rushed. It paid off. They were indeed fortunate and pleased with the results. Some of their experiences were soft, baffling breezes out of nowhere, fast-moving light, orbs, and melodic music in the distance. They all agreed that dawn and dusk were the most fruitful periods. I'm sorry to have missed that trip!

3. Sound

As mentioned, the fairy lives on a level slightly above the earth called the ethereal plane, but they have the ability to travel back and forth easily. Consequently, the voice of the fairy, given it decides to speak, is much different from the human voice. The vocal sound is very high-pitched yet audible. It is possible for a human to hear the fairy's voice but not recognize it as that of a fairy. Moreover, fairies communicate through lighthearted whispering, faint bell sounds, or music. If you travel through the woods or any isolated natural setting, don't be startled if you suddenly hear melodies in the distance. It is possible to discern fairy music since fairy music is more melodious than human music, and the tunes are written by the fairies themselves. Therefore, the selections played or sung will be unrecognizable. Human music will have a familiarity and resonate with you immediately, whereas fairy music will be pleasantly haunting.

4. Sensation

When a fairy is present, an exhilarating feeling overcomes your body, comparable to the emotions experienced when a very happy event or surprise takes place. Fairies present themselves with a floral scent, a quick chill in the air, or the feeling that something brushed by us. As fairies connect with our "feeling" sense, their presence may be felt by a pulsation on the skin or a feeling of being watched in a dark room or out in the wild. Pay attention!

5. Random Fairy Communication

Fairies have fun and try to connect with us by casually hiding objects. They adore flashy things and tend to move items that glitter, especially jewelry. When I lived in Pennsylvania, this happened to me often. I adore bling! One week my rhinestone earrings and other shiny items moved from place to place. I knew it wasn't my husband pulling a gag, as his personality doesn't lean toward those types of hijinks. Finally, those earrings disappeared altogether but reappeared a few days later in my pantry! I don't cook, so it was bizarre I found them at all. It's helpful to speak to fairies at times like these and urge them to return the article. I didn't speak to them on that occasion but will next time.

The fairy is a fun-loving, mischievous sort. Below are a few ways they may innocently try to connect with human life:

- Refrigerated and unexpired creamer may suddenly turn bad.
- A pet may act suddenly uncomfortable, as if sensing something different is around.
- A gentle, inexplicable breeze blows out of nowhere and touches you.

Fairies also may be invited into your space. One way is to summon them telepathically. First, be seated quietly in a place with no distractions. If you wish, add flowers, flute music, and special twilight lighting. Next, visualize yourself surrounded by a ball of white, sparkly light, with fairies immersing you in magical fairy dust. Then, imagine your feet like tree roots, connecting down to the center of the earth's core. This will ground and connect you to Mother Earth. Finally, speak to these special entities as you would a friend. Feel free to ask anything. Then, pay close attention to any random thoughts, feelings, or images you receive. These will only be of love and guidance. Disregard anything other than pleasing thoughts. Let your sixth sense come into play. At the close of the session, send a thank-you their way. Furthermore, show your support by doing a fairylike deed, such as caring for an animal in need or picking up some trash in your neighborhood.

Fairies are more apt to assist and appear when you do the following:

- Believe.
- Have an accepting heart.
- Demonstrate true love to animals and others.
- Exhibit real affection for the environment.
- Do not litter.
- Care for plants, trees, and shrubbery.
- Avoid using pesticides.
- Exist truthfully as a caring and loving citizen.
- Enjoy life. Play and sing as often as possible.
- Seek assistance with your gardening or pets when necessary.
- Make a special place in your yard or home, and invite them in.
- Try to tune into them. (Be receptive. They will respond and come near.)

For optimal results, plan a fairy excursion, as my associates did. First, find a suitable area, whether at home or in nature. Then, mentally say hello to the fairies and ask their permission to communicate. Every being deserves respect. You must be full of good intentions but also must be polite. They will not reveal themselves so that you can ridicule or mock them. Fairies will be very attuned to your energy and can pick up on your true thoughts and vibrations, and they will evaluate your worthiness.

Hold a sparkly or shiny object—they love such things and will be attracted. Holding a crystal also may invoke them. Pay attention to your feelings. Since peripheral vision is more attuned to movement, I tend to look for things out of the corner of my eye. Try taking photos so you might have proof you witnessed fairy light or movement—or simply to immortalize the adventure. I don't recommend using a cell phone but rather a digital camera. Honestly, you may miss something due to the limited resolution of the cell phone. The digital camera can seize fairies' quick energy. As mentioned earlier, choose a natural setting with many trees, as fairies love to jump from leaf to leaf. The city is not a prudent setting to snap pics, as the metropolitan lighting may confuse or muddy your findings. A fairy may be hanging out there, but in the wild is a more obvious choice to connect.

As you are taking the picture, you won't notice anything in the viewfinder, but you may see the results in the photographs. It's a sign you have taken a true fairy shot when light spots or circles are visible in the photo. These are different from the solid ghostly orb, as they will appear in an oval shape and in colors such as blue or purple.

Photo sessions can be fun and don't have to be done in silence or when you're alone. Make a mental note of the feelings you experience. Later, write notes about the contact you made, especially for comparison if you plan to do more outings in the future. Jot down all thoughts and feelings you received. The fairies are healers, so they may wish to impart vital information.

Plan ahead, and do not rush your excursion. Make an appointment with yourself and the fairies. They will know you're coming. Carve out special time especially for this purpose. Be aware of all the signs you have been given.

Please do not criticize yourself and hold high expectations the very time first time. As with everything in life, practice makes perfect. Plus, it's a fun experience to repeat. The more experiences you have, the better you will will become. Just a tip: Fairies are especially lively during the solstice and equinox periods.

Remember to always send a thank-you to the fairies for their hospitality at the close of any communication session, just as you would to people who invited you into their homes.

Connect with the Use of Crystals

Another simple way to make contact with the fairies is through the use of natural crystals. Countless positive accomplishments can be made with the proper use of these stones. It is important to not to use man-made crystals to connect with our nature guardians. The power lies with nature's true minerals. Crystals hold powerful energy and are supportive when trying to get in touch with fairies. Using crystals while stating an optimistic affirmation is a stronger technique for creating the celestial exchange. An affirmation, in the basic sense, is a statement repeated each day or over and over until it becomes a reality. The affirmer must truly believe in what he or she is professing in order to manifest it into certainty.

I recommend practicing the following eight steps when you intend to bond with the fairy:

1. Begin in a nature setting, if possible. This may be simply outside in nature or in your fairy garden. It doesn't have to be elaborate.
2. Select the crystal(s) that call to you and hold between both palms. Gaze at the crystals and hold only positive intentions.
3. Inhale deeply though the nose, and exhale three times through the mouth. Breathe in positivity in and push out all negativity.
4. Introduce yourself to the fairies. Ask permission to communicate. For example, "Hello, my name is _____. I wish to speak with you. I hope this meets your approval." This is only a general guide. Feel free to use your own wording.
5. Affirm. A sample sentence would be, "I connect positively with my very guardians every day."

6. Focus. Relax. Gather information.
7. At the close of the session, express gratitude.
8. As soon as possible, journal all findings. Journal pages are available at the end of this book for your convenience.

I have included eight of my favorite crystal recommendations below. It is advisable to hold a few of your choice stones at the same time, as each is known to have different benefits.

1. Fairy stone

   The fairy stone has a point on one end and tiny crystals on the other. This is one of my favorites, and I think it's very cool-looking since it resembles a wand.

2. Tourmaline

   Tourmaline is a protective stone and helps with grounding. It also transmutes negative thoughts into positive ones.

3. Green tourmaline (verdelite)

   Green tourmaline assists with conducting visualization. It is a natural, powerful healer and has been said to help heal plant life if placed in close proximity to it.

4. Harlequin quartz

   This stone promotes inspiration. It links the spiritual and physical worlds together. In addition, it aids in the emotional healing of the heart after a breakup.

5. Bloodstone

   Bloodstone is a healing crystal. It boosts the immune system and reduces irritability.

6. Jade

   Jade symbolizes purity and serenity and protects against danger. It's so pretty and useful.

7. Prehnite

   Prehnite protects the aura. Imagine it as a warrior's shield or an umbrella in the rain. It is a very helpful stone to hold while meditating.

8. Turquoise

   Turquoise signifies passage between worlds, such as the earth plane and heaven. It protects, heals, and heightens communication. This stone is well-regarded by the Native Americans. Personally, I highly respect any recommendations Native Americans offer, as they are such highly spiritual, powerful people.

   Once a connection is made with the fairies, you will know it instantly! A feeling of a higher consciousness and new awareness will overcome you. Plus, a newfound caring and responsibility to the planet will arise. In fact, an individual who newly connects may feel an urge to engage in some or all of the following activities:

   o   Pick up litter. (Please wear gloves.)
   o   Participate in environmental projects or, on a smaller scale, practice little things, such as committing to using eco-friendly bags or other items.
   o   Create a personalized fairy garden.
   o   Consume healthier and more natural foods.
   o   Carve out a garden space to grow organic vegetables.
   o   Adopt or foster a pet; offer personal time at a shelter.
   o   Volunteer for a children's mission.

Try any or all of the activities for yourself. You may see, feel, hear, and sense many new things. Perhaps you already have but did not realize it!

Overall, each week make it a quest to spend more time outside in a serene area, near flowers or shrubbery, especially at dawn and/or dusk. Likewise, the equinox and the solstice are highly important times to the fairy. Legend has it that fairies will not be seen by humankind in bright daylight; rather, their shimmer can be seen at night or on overcast days.

Fairies, our naure's keepers, are carefree beings who do not care for the obvious but enjoy the unexpected. They relish in their privacy and will only allow you to see, feel, and hear them as they wish. I would bet if you haven't noticed a fairy already, you will soon. When it happens, you will feel very honored!

The fairies are passionate environmentalists. As we give to them, they, in turn, will provide for us. They are famous for leaving gifts and positive signs and for ushering new opportunities into the lives of the hopeful. Inviting them into your life is great fun. You likely will enjoy discovering and becoming familiar with the fairy existence. I find that daily life is more entertaining and has more sparkle with the fairies in it.

Nothing can be truer than fairy wisdom. It is as true as sunbeams.

—Douglas William Jerrold

Chapter 5

THE TOOTH FAIRY

Losing baby teeth were a part and parcel of one's life—a symbol of growing up, and it is the tooth-fairy that makes this otherwise dreaded and painful process an exciting one—something to look forward to.

—Mansi Maheshwari

The tooth fairy is very near and dear to my heart. She is a well-recognized, yet imaginary, fairy who deserves an important place in this book. I'll refer to the tooth fairy as female in gender, as that's the way I have always known her. Some believe the tooth fairy is a woman, while others recognize the tooth fairy as genderless or even male. Whatever your belief, the tooth fairy is sheer magic!

In the United States, when a child's tooth falls out, it is customary for the youngster to place it under his or her pillow, knowing cash will be delivered to him or her by morning. The generosity of the tooth fairy's payment for the collection of the tooth varies. It depends on many factors, such as age of the child, area of residence and the annual income and education level of the family. She is a good compass of how the United States is trending economically.

In an article in *USA Today* (2017), Mina Hag shared results of Delta Dental's thirteenth annual Tooth Fairy Survey, conducted in 2016, noting, "Last year, the Tooth Fairy paid about $290.6 million in the U.S. for lost teeth, a 13.5% increase from 2015. Cash payouts for a first lost tooth are up about 10% to $5.72. First-tooth payouts are typically higher than average."

The tooth fairy seems to give according to salary levels across the USA. The following is how the tooth fairy spreads the wealth, from lowest to highest: the Midwest, the southern states, the Northeast, and the West, as the top of the line! It's interesting that countrywide, fathers are more generous than mothers. (Oops. I meant to say the tooth fairy, not Dad and Mom.)

Of course, this is just an average. I have found parents do lavish their children with twenty dollars or more in exchange for a tooth.

Visa offers an online "Tooth Fairy Calculator," which provides an idea of the average amount parents offer. This calculator is also available as a download and on the Facebook apps page. (The technology today is amazing, right?) When my son, Ian, was tooth-fairy age, I gave what I believed was reasonable for the time. I never compared rates with other parents or read studies of what was being given in my area. Was I foolish? I can see now that the tooth fairy was always generous to Ian, probably better than the Visa study at that point in time. Ian, being a good saver, unlike his mother, probably has his tooth money today!

On the website McClatchy DC Bureau, Lindsay Wise (2015) quoted Nat Sillin, Visa's director of global financial education, who reported, "One of the reasons Visa does the survey is to encourage parents to teach their children about saving and budgeting." He felt the decline in the tooth fee is "reasonable and prudent."

Recently, the parents with whom I have spoken have reasoned that offering money or even a small gift makes it more pleasurable for the youth who has lost a tooth. The mothers and fathers added that they often feel pressured to leave as much or even more money than their contemporaries.

According to the American legend, the tooth fairy automatically senses when a child loses a tooth and schedules to fly into the child's bedroom that very night. The tooth is placed under the youngster's pillow, and the fairy takes it and leaves a monetary feel-better present. Her presence is never detected. Today, rather than possibly disturbing the child's sleep when the money is placed under the pillow, some families opt for fancy boxes or special separate tooth pillows. In the United States, that is the standard operating procedure. In other countries, presents are left instead of cash. That's a nice idea as well. In the event the child loses or swallows the tooth, the tooth fairy is kind and rewards the child anyway—very sweet.

It is up for speculation when the tooth fairy first came onto the scene in the United States, but she's been a recognizable figure in the United States since the late 1920s. My grandmother, who moved from Ireland to the US in the early 1900s, claimed that the tooth fairy was new to the scene back then. Her father was a businessman in Manhattan at that time. He had heard of children receiving money for their teeth from a mysterious woman with wings while they slept. He liked the idea and decided to slip a bit of cash or small gifts under his daughter's pillow as well. New York City is always cutting edge.

In Europe, the concept of the tooth fairy goes back to the Middle Ages. In parts of Europe, when the child's tooth fell out, it would be buried. After a few teeth were lost, the child would then receive a gift. Long ago in Northern Europe, the practice was to issue a tooth fee (money given to the child who lost the tooth) but only when the first tooth was lost. This concept was recorded in the earliest written record of Norse and Northern European traditions. In the Spanish-speaking countries, a mouse named *Ratoncito Perez* collected the children's lost teeth. Similarly, in France, children believe a mouse, *La Petite Souris*, acts as the tooth fairy in animal form, not as a female fairy, as in our society. It seems in almost every culture there exists some tradition surrounding children's naturally lost teeth. It is a widely practiced ritual in this world. The United States, France, and Spanish-speaking countries aren't the only countries that have a tooth-fairy tradition; Russia, New Zealand, and Mexico do as well. In the days of the Vikings, they would exchange money for children's teeth.

Listed below are additional ways children in other lands celebrate losing teeth:

- South Africa: The tooth is placed in a slipper, not under the pillow.
- Iraq, Egypt: The child's tooth is tossed toward the sky.
- Asian countries: The upper teeth are pitched onto the floor, while the lower teeth are thrown toward the roof. Wishes are made while launching the tooth.
- Central Asia: The tooth is buried by a tree or sometimes fed to a dog. The rationale is the new tooth will be very strong like the dog's teeth or the tree root.

My grandmother Nell provided much fun and valuable information to me on one of my favorite subjects, the tooth fairy. The phrase *tooth fee* was popular years ago, meaning that money would be exchanged for the tooth. The term *tooth fairy*, according to my grandmother's vast knowledge, was coined by a small child who could not pronounce the phrase "tooth fee" and instead said "tooth fairy." Sounds plausible. Who can be really be sure? It's one of the many mysteries of life. Folklore is so enjoyable.

Why all the hoopla involving the tooth fairy? I personally believe the tooth fairy is a wonderful invention. For a child, the thought of losing a tooth can be a frightening experience. Yet the image of a fantastical being as a generous fairy or magical mouse arriving to collect the tooth and exchange it for cash certainly makes the scenario much brighter! When I was a child, I remember thinking, *What's this all about? Why can't we all keep our teeth?* It was daunting for a young mind. Yet a sense of relief came over me because my grandmother spoke so highly of the trusted tooth fairy. Of course, money also speaks volumes.

How can a parent make the experience even more fun? You may be thinking right now, *Isn't money enough?* Some parents prefer not to leave the tooth under the pillow since it is very hard to make the switch without waking the child. In that case, using a decorative box or separate tooth pillow are nice options. I've been known to leave glitter on the rug, proving the tooth fairy has been on the premises. Friends have left notes from the tooth fairy, praising the child for good hygiene. It's fun to use your ingenuity, and you and your child will remember the event always.

Many moons ago, when I was tooth-fairy age, I asked my mother if she thought the tooth fairy could leave a handwritten note for me in sparkly gold ink when she collected my tooth. I believed my mother had a special connection with the tooth fairy, so naturally my request would definitely be communicated to her. After all, my grandmother and mother spoke of the tooth fairy as a close friend. In those days, sparkly pens were virtually unheard of. Yet I had complete confidence that the tooth fairy would possess one since she is magical. What do you know? The morning after my tooth was retrieved, I received money and a handwritten letter addressed to me, written in sparkly ink! I did think that her handwriting resembled my mother's, but I quickly dismissed that thought. I was so excited! To this day, that is still a truly happy memory to me. I still wonder how my mother did it. At that time, we lived in a rural area and specialty craft stores did not exist. Magic does exist!

We know that the child places his or her tooth under the pillow, but what happens after the sweet fairy takes the tooth? My mother told me that the tooth fairy magically turns the tooth into a star! That's why there are so many beautiful, twinkling stars in the sky. I always loved that explanation.

Years ago, when my niece, Rowena, was tooth-fairy age, her father (my brother) certainly did not possess the clever knack that my mother possessed. Rowena had lost a tooth and placed it out for the tooth fairy. The next morning, a check was left in exchange for her tooth. It was endorsed by my brother. What? So many thoughts went through her little mind. Does the tooth fairy work for my father? Is there a tooth fairy at all? It was ridiculous of my brother to leave a check, but that's the way he is. My mother quickly remedied the situation expertly with her magical imagination. All was well with little Rowena and in the land of the tooth fairy once again.

It is an ingigma, but did you know the United States celebrates the tooth fairy each year on February 28? Additionally, she is commemorated again on August 22. That's buckets of merriment, but she deserves such attention. After all, each year the tooth fairy effortlessly carries money and teeth without a vacation. The good news continues! In the event you celebrate her holiday on February 28, it may be combined with National Chocolate Soufflé Day. You may satisfy your sweet tooth and celebrate the tooth fairy at the same time! I know what I'm doing next February 28!

Overall, the tooth fairy is an icon in society who offers comfort to our little ones. She rewards those brave souls every day across the land who are missing a tooth after it was swallowed, yanked, or lost naturally. Whoever said being a kid is easy? The tooth fairy is here to offer comfort and joy. She has for many years, and it sounds like she will be sticking around. That's a worthy broadcast!

Other than a dimple in a cute little chin,
What's more adorable than a toothless grin?

—Terri Guillemets

Chapter 6

FAMOUS FAIRIES

If you see the magic in a fairy tale, you can face the future.

—Danielle Steel

In fairyland, there are various fairies of note in addition to the famous tooth fairy. This chapter is dedicated to those personalities who add so much delight to our lives through literary works, dramatic stage performances, and Hollywood movies. Sit back, relax, and let me entertain you.

Noteworthy fairies include the Blue Fairy, the fairy godmother, Finvarra and Oonagh, Oberon and Titania, sugar plum fairies, and Tinker Bell.

The Blue Fairy

The Blue Fairy originated from the Enchanted Forest. She is famous for granting wishes to those in need, but the individual must make the plea, silently or aloud, in order to acquire a wish come true. The Blue Fairy must be called on for support.

Most people probably connect the Blue Fairy with Walt Disney's popular 1940 film *Pinocchio*. Walt Disney portrayed this fairy as a human-sized, beautiful female who wears a shimmering blue dress. Wherever she travels, she carries her wish-fulfilling wand.

This fairy tale focuses on Geppetto, who makes a wish upon a star that his beloved wooden marionette would turn into a living, breathing human boy. The Blue Fairy hears his appeal for help and grants Geppetto's desire by using her magic wand to transform his marionette into a living boy. The Blue Fairy only granted his wish because she believed Geppetto had brought so much happiness to others.

Do you recall the song "When You Wish Upon a Star"? This was written for this 1940 movie and is played at the beginning of the movie. As a child, I adored wishing upon a star each evening. Truthfully, every now and then, I still do!

The Fairy Godmother

The fairy godmother is recognized as a motherly fairy figure with magical powers. Typically, she is depicted as a plain, middle-aged or sometimes older woman, with white hair and a stocky build. The fairy godmother is clearly not characterized as the pretty version of the fairy. She watches closely over younger children and is very gentle, kind, and supportive—and sometimes forgetful.

Walt Disney popularized the fairy godmother in the 1953 film *Cinderella* and the 1959 Disney film *Sleeping Beauty*. Sleeping Beauty, also known as Princess Aurora, was lucky enough to have three fairy godmothers!

The fairy godmother is also in the 2004 movie *Shrek 2*, produced by DreamWorks Animation. In this movie, however, she is portrayed as a self-centered fairy, not the typical sweet and caring fairy godmother. Even though DreamWorks gave the fairy godmother a different twist than Disney, I found *Shrek 2* to be a very entertaining movie.

Oberon and Titania

Folklore relates there is indeed a king and queen who rule over the fairies. In the sixteenth century, William Shakespeare popularized this idea in his play *A Midsummer Night's Dream*. Oberon is the king of all fairies, and his queen is named Titania. Titania cares for and loves a changeling baby. The king becomes jealous of her attention toward the baby, and this leads to major scuffles between them. Their fighting is so intense that its negativity results in weather mishaps, causing strong winds, floods, and famine. The married royal couple spars like many other couples do, yet Titania's mood is able to alter the weather in a disastrous way. I believe Shakespeare was on to something. Could some of our major storms be caused by the high level of negativity present in the world today?

Finvarra and Oonagh

Finvarra and Oonagh are a married couple who are considered fairy nobility. In ancient Irish folklore, they are the high king and queen of all fairies.

Finvarra, the high king of the fairy realm, is connected to the "wee people," the leprechauns. He is regarded as a kind king who comes to the aid of those who require his help. Finvarra's specialty is helping with the farm—healthy crops and horses, good harvests, and abundance. In return, he appreciates assistance when he needs it.

Finvarra is a very powerful king and has great influence over others. He is a heavy partier and not loyal to his wife, Oonagh. He is promiscuous, has a roving eye, and entertains both fairy and mortal women.

Oonagh, the queen of the fairies, is a truly gorgeous being and is illustrated with beautiful, long, wavy blonde hair. Oonagh, beautiful but sad, has been deceived by her husband, the mighty king, on numerous occasions. It is said that due to his betrayal, Oonagh has the power to hear the call from any being who needs to heal from hurt and pain due to a betrayal in a relationship.

Sugar Plum Fairies

Sugar plum fairies are known for their love of dance and sweets. Sugar plum fairies adore hanging out in an orchard or plum grove. The sugar plum fairy's favorite holiday is Christmas. We frequently see their images during the holidays in gift shops and on decorations.

Sugar plum fairies were made legendary in the ballet, *The Nutcracker*, with a score by Russian composer Pyotr Ilyich Tchaikovsky. Due to his famous "Dance of the Sugar Plum Fairy," this fairy became unforgettable. Tchaikovsky created a tinkling sound from an instrument called the celesta, which looks similar to a small piano. This sweet, tinkling melody lent itself very well to the fairy persona and created the perfect mood for the audience.

Tinker Bell

Tinker Bell is an iconic fairy—everyone seems to know who she is. Tinker Bell is the amazing creation of the author James M. Barrie in his famous book *Peter Pan*.

Later, Disney created an adaptation of Tinker Bell. She is referred to as Tink or Miss Bell. Tink is a cute, spirited yet jealous little fairy. She is Peter Pan's buddy who endeared herself to him and led Peter through multiple journeys. Tink sports a green outfit and a magic wand. She has blonde hair and flies through the air. I'd guess she's one of Disney's most recognizable characters. In my opinion, because of Walt Disney, she has raised fairy awareness and popularity immensely. Thankfully, Tink has had a huge impact on the exposure of magical beings.

Below are a few fairy-believing authors who have promoted fairy life through their works:

1. Alexander Pope (1688–1744)
   Alexander Pope was an English poet and satirical writer. Pope wrote lovely passages idealizing fairies, with the exception of jokingly making a derogatory remark about deceased socialites who possessed fairies in order to live on and not give up their earthly pleasures.

2. Sir Walter Scott (1771–1832)
   Sir Walter Scott was a Scottish playwright and poet. He was a judge by profession who parlayed his experiences into his writings. Clever! He was also a historical novelist. Scott believed the land of the fairies was a beautiful place.

3. William Shakespeare (1564–1616)
   Shakespeare was an actor, playwright, and English poet during the late sixteenth and early seventeenth centuries. He's often considered the finest author the English language has ever recognized. He popularized the term *fairy* in many of his writings. Shakespeare promoted the "wee people" as playful and mischievous but not harmful.

   The "Bard of Avon" was a common term used for Shakespeare. Bard denotes poet. Avon indicates the part of England Shakespeare was born and buried, Stratford-upon-Avon.

4. William Butler Yeats (1865–1939)
   Yeats was an Irish poet who won the Nobel Prize. Fairy folklore influenced his ideas, writings, and poetry. He passionately believed in the concept of fairies, as did his ancestors. He also held a solid belief in the supernatural forces in the world.

It is wonderful that so many literary giants have put the fairy in the spotlight. Their works have been read for generations. Today we are able to spread the word ourselves about the fairy realm. I believe that these writers must have had a deep belief in fairies to have created such fanciful literary works.

Hand in hand, with fairy grace,
Will we sing and bless this place.

—William Shakespeare
A Midsummer Night's Dream

Chapter 7

FAIRY TALE VERSUS FOLKLORE

If you want your children to be intelligent, read them fairy tales. If you want them to be more intelligent, read them more fairy tales.

—Albert Einstein

Fairy tales and folklore hold a prominent place in nearly every society and culture. As a child, you may have been told fantastical stories, some of which took place hundreds of years ago and others as far back as thousands of years past. Did you realize there is a difference between a fairy tale and folklore? The terms *fairy tale* and *folklore* are not interchangeable; they do have similarities but also distinct differences.

The Fairy Tale

A fairy tale is a story passed down through the generations that has been romanticized. It is a more glamorous account that surrounds a mythical being like a fairy, elf, unicorn, witch, dragon, mermaid, or princess. The main character, a human, encounters a struggle, only to be saved by a presence with magical powers. In the end, a lesson must be learned. It is a fiction-based story and related to children's literature.

A few fine examples of fairy tales are *Cinderella, The Elves and the Shoemaker, The Emperor's New Clothes*, and *The Frog Prince.*

Cinderella has many variations. One of the most popular versions was written by Charles Perrault in 1698, but it has had many adaptations over the years. The Brothers Grimm wrote one version in 1812, and Walt Disney produced an animated film in 1950. In the modern version, a beautiful girl is controlled and treated wickedly by her malicious stepmother. This stepmother prevents her from attending the ball she so desperately wishes to attend. Her two mean stepsisters are allowed to go. A fairy godmother appears to Cinderella and uses happy magic to save the day. Cinderella is in attendance and meets a handsome prince. She can only stay until midnight and dashes out of the party quickly, only to lose her slipper. It is found by the prince who uses it to locate Cinderella. After much trouble, his efforts pay off and the handsome prince is successful. They marry and live happily ever after.

Perrault's seventeenth-century version and Walt Disney's *Cinderella* mention a fairy godmother. The Brothers Grimm do not. Rather, a bird from a magical tree supports the young lady. *Cinderella* was also performed as a French opera, *Cendrillon*, created by Jules Massenet, which premiered in Paris in 1899.

The Elves and the Shoemaker was written by the Brothers Grimm. A few different adaptations exist. The story centers around a flat-broke shoemaker and his wife. One day, this cobbler runs completely out of materials and is unable to purchase any new supplies. He and his wife go to bed feeling very dismal. The next day when they wake, they discover new shoes have been made. This is baffling to the shoemaker and his spouse. Yet when a very wealthy man offers to buy the expertly made shoes, the shoemaker sells them and is happy to be financially comfortable again. After that, new and exquisitely handcrafted shoes are made over the next two nights, and the shoemaker does not understand how this is happening. Naturally curious, one night the shoemaker and his wife spy and notice that elves are fashioning the new shoes. Ever so grateful, he and his wife sew garments for the elves so they have winter clothing. The elves are thankful, feel their good deed has been done, and move on to help other unfortunate folks.

The Emperor's New Clothes, written by Hans Christian Anderson, depicts a narcissistic emperor who only cares about his appearance. The emperor pays two weavers to craft a very fine outfit for him. They outwit him by explaining that the emperor's new ensemble will appear invisible to anyone who is unintelligent, beneath his stature, or not fit to do their jobs. In reality, there is no outfit—the emperor is not wearing any clothes! Everyone pretends to see the emperor's new outfit for fear of offending the emperor or looking stupid or unfit. Finally, an unassuming child professes that the emperor is not wearing any garments. Until then, the conceited emperor had been riding in a parade and feeling self-assured in his new clothes that the weavers had made. Even though the emperor realized he had been duped, he continued with the procession, despite the bad news. Only in a fairy tale, right?

The Frog Prince, also by the Brothers Grimm, is the story of a talking frog who was once a human prince. A malicious sorceress cast a foul spell on the prince and turned him into a frog. Later on, when a bratty princess loses her golden ball in a pond, the frog is quick to offer to get it for her—but first he has conditions the princess must meet. Before he will retrieve the ball, she must let the frog eat from her plate, be his friend, and allow him to sleep on her pillow. The princess heartily agrees. After she is given her precious ball, she flees to the castle. The frog appears there, but she is not interested in fulfilling the agreement. Her father. however, forces the princess to keep her word. Disgusted, she agrees. After a few nights on her pillow, the frog transforms into a handsome young price, and she is delighted. They marry and leave immediately for his kingdom. *The Frog Prince* accurately follows the blueprint of a fairy tale. It is an extravagantly written story in which the make-believe main character has a conflict and is then saved by a magical character.

Aren't fairy tales fun? Who doesn't adore a little magic mixed with a drama-filled situation that then results in a happy ending?

Melissa Taylor (2012) reported in her article, "8 Reasons Why Fairy Tales are Essential to Childhood," that fairy tales are indeed a positive influence in a child's life. Through her studies, she developed the following points to explain her rationale for why it is important for children to be exposed to fairy tales:

1. Fairy tales show kids how to handle problems.
2. Fairy tales build emotional resiliency.
3. Fairy tales give us a common language.
4. Fairy tales cross cultural boundaries.
5. Fairy tales teach a story.
6. Fairy tales develop a child's imagination.
7. Fairy tales give parents opportunities to teach critical thinking skills.
8. Fairy tales teach lessons.

I agree that fairy tales are important to children. They ignite a creativity and make the world an enchanting, imaginary experience. I am the youngest of five children and remember hearing many fairy tales. Yet a friend, who was the youngest of six children, mentioned she hardly knew of any fairy tales. Her mother admitted that by the time she was born, she was "fairy taled out."

Folklore

Folklore has been present for thousands and thousands of years and is passed down from generation to generation, often in the oral tradition. Folklore is recognized in almost every culture; every society has its own unique stories to tell. Over time, because folklore is often communicated orally, it can become like the old game "Operator," where children sit in a line or in a circle, and the first child whispers a message to the next child in line. This process is followed until it reaches the last youngster. Then, the last child recites the message out loud as he or she heard it. By the time the message reaches the end, it is usually radically different from the original declaration—and folklore can be like that. The stories told from one generation to the next may become distorted or embellished over time through word of mouth, but that adds to the merriment. The story is as good as the last person who told it.

Folklore surrounds real-life events with human characters, while in fairy tales, there is usually a level of suffering and lessons to be learned.

Numerous folktales exist all across the globe. The following is a small sampling:

Trolls

In Scandinavian folklore, trolls are described as small, hairy, supernatural beings. They move slowly and are supposedly unintelligent. These creatures are very peaceful unless threatened. Others claim certain trolls are as human-looking as you and me. Trolls reside far away from humankind in their own civilizations. They are interested in gold and store it on mountaintops, under bridges, or in bodies of water. Trolls are frightened of lightning and church bells.

Kraken

The Norse believe the kraken is a huge sea creature, reminiscent of the octopus. It has spearlike tentacles, and it horrified sailors and devoured their ships. The kraken also played a part in natural disasters, such as volcanic activity.

Hulder

A hulder is part of Scandinavian folklore and exists mainly in Denmark, Norway, and Sweden. A hulder is a striking woman with long, gorgeous hair and a tail. This malicious temptress will lure men into the forest to steal their souls. She is a shape-shifter who may hide her tail from her prey. It is said if a man weds a hulder in a church, she will lose her tail but also her beauty.

Toni Klein

Changeling

A changeling in folklore is a descendant of an elf, fairy, or other mystical creature. A fairy steals a human baby and replaces the child with his or her offspring. Later, the human parents discover inexplicable physical and/or mental disorders in the baby, which they think is their human child. Why the switch? The fairy may want the human child to become a servant in fairyland, or the fairy may want a human to care for his or her fairy child, or the fairy might just want a human baby.

Films, novels, plays, and television productions have featured the changeling, including the following:

- *The Changeling*, a 1898 novel by Sir Walter Besant
- *The Changeling*, a 1974 television drama

Interestingly enough, "The Changeling" was the title of an episode of the 1970s television series *The Waltons*.

Fairy tales, handed down in written form, are said to trace back thousands of years, but folklore may predate fairy tales, since folklore is passed down orally. On a similar note, both fairy tales and folklore are entertaining and may provide hours of enjoyment for you, your children, and others. Depending on the story, it could be scary or pleasing. Watch the content. Not all children enjoy a good thrill.

Every time a child says "I don't believe in fairies," there
is a little fairy somewhere that falls down dead.

—James M. Barrie, *Peter Pan*

Chapter 8

FAIRY SIGHTINGS

Those who don't believe in magic will never find it.

—Roald Dahl

As a fairyologist and staunch fairy believer, I realize fairies exist all over the continent. Yet many people think that fairies congregate only in areas such as Iceland (elves), the UK, and, of course, Ireland (leprechauns). Ireland readily comes to everyone's mind when they think of wee folk abounding. Fairies, however, also have been mentioned in the folklore of less-considered areas, such as the USA, South Africa, and other Western civilizations. Most nations have a common passion for the belief in the mysterious. Could it be that fairies are not more popular in Ireland but that the belief in them is more accepted there, and it's commonplace to openly discuss them?

A few years ago, I visited Ireland. One of my great desires was to spot a leprechaun. Most of my time, however, was spent in Dublin, a well-populated city with many college students. In all the hustle and bustle, I missed seeing one. On a happier note, however, I did capture some interesting things on film. I was snapping away on my throwaway camera while in the city, but then I left to explore the countryside.

Later, after the film was developed, I noticed the pictures I had taken on my excursion, especially those taken in the countryside, were full of shimmery orbs. I had never had that experience before. I'm grateful the Irish fairies were communicating with me. Unfortunately, years later, those photos were ruined when Hurricane Sandy hit New Jersey.

Below, I have detailed a few cases regarding fairies who have interacted with humans around the world, including Ireland, Iceland, the UK, and the USA.

Dublin Castle, Dublin, Ireland

Fairies—the "good people" or "good folk," as they are called in Ireland—are everywhere. The fairy trails and hills at Dublin Castle are especially highly populated. Old-timers warn to never venture directly into the hills or step within a fairy ring. Those who have been bold enough to try have suffered for their actions. Some folks have dared to tamper with a hill by digging its dirt. Others have knowingly danced in a fairy ring. This is not good behavior and is discouraged. Legend says that those who do may suffer physically afterward, or death may even result.

I recall a similar situation when my husband and I visited Scotland. A young man on our tour, after being warned, purposefully hopped in and out of a ring and laughed. I felt so uncomfortable, and to this day I still wonder about the fate of that gentleman. I hope he was given a pass. The bottom line is to treat the fairies as you would like to be treated—with courtesy, respect, and a caring for their land and possessions. We are all beings with feelings who appreciate kindness and respect for our personal quarters.

Iceland

Iceland holds a high regard for and belief in the elf. Folklore is very powerful in Iceland. The elves, or "hidden people," reside below the earth's surface under huge rocks. Engineers have held serious discussions on rerouting a highway around the residence of an elf family. Developers will not build new construction in the dwelling areas. Icelanders wish to live in harmony with the elf population, not to disturb them. Last year, my niece Rowena visited Iceland. She mentioned that the tourists loved to hear of the Icelanders' beliefs. I am fully on board with the philosophy of not disturbing the elves. No human would care to be uprooted; it's the same for elves.

Those who have spotted elves in Iceland say they are very similar to humans in appearance—not like Santa's helpers, as the media would have us believe. To Icelanders, the primary differences between humans and elves is the clothes they wear. The elves' garments have an outdated appearance, as if the clothes are over 150 years old. Their height is another factor; their approximate height is three feet.

Lancashire, England

Jill Reilly (2015), "Away with the Fairies" university lecturer, claims to have photographed real-life tiny Tinker Bells flying through the air in the British countryside. John Hyatt, of Manchester Metropolitan University in England, claims he captured fairies on film. Hyatt insists his pictures are the real deal and not altered in any way, thereby illustrating that fairy life in the countryside of Rossendale Valley, Lancashire, does exist.

The Cottingley Fairies
Cottingley, England

In 1917, two young girls, Elsie and Frances, who were cousins borrowed a camera. They reported that they had captured five separate images of fairies on film. These photos were taken where the two had been outside playing. At first the sightings were thought to be legitimate. The news of fairy photographs especially piqued the interest of one particular writer, who was penning an article on fairies for a magazine. This author Sir Arthur Conan Doyle, creator of Sherlock Holmes. Doyle was exceedingly enthused and viewed this as affirmation that fairies were real. He wished to share this evidence with the world. After his article was published, the reviews were mixed, as some citizens were accepting and others were not. It wasn't until 1983 that the two girls, now elderly women, revealed it was a hoax—that the four photos had been falsified and were pictures taken of cutouts of fairies. This was disappointing news to many who had taken interest in the case. However, Frances claimed until her death that the fifth and last photograph was indeed real.

In the United States, some folks have faith in the little people population as well.

North Carolina

The Cherokee tribe of the North Carolina mountains believe in fairies, known as the "little people." During their time spent in the mountains, members have spotted different types of fairies. They have described them and developed categories for each.

The Laurel People

Laurels may be either nice or naughty; thankfully, the friendly Laurels comprise most of the population. They receive joy in others' happiness and care about the countryside and its animals. The mischievous Laurels, however, are the sort who engage in foolery and trick the hunters. From time to time, mysterious stones fly out of nowhere and strike them. This usually occurs only if the huntsman arbitrarily take an object belonging to the mountain without permission.

The Rock People

This is a hostile group that likes its own space and does not appreciate interlopers. If anyone trespasses on their space, the Rock People feel the need to get even. Trappers who have ventured onto Rock People's land have become delirious and lose their way in the woods. If and when they do arrive back at camp, they have limited memory of what transpired within the last few hours. The message is to respect individuals and the boundaries of others.

The Dogwood People

Dogwoods are good through and through. They exhibit love and joy to all. No hijinks or harm ever occurs.

As a group overall, the little people are generally kind folk who are very fond of privacy. They guard the environment and its wildlife. These fairies are described as little men and women, approximately three feet tall, with black, white, or golden skin and moon-shaped eyes.

Mount Shasta, California

Mount Shasta is a very interesting and energetic place. It is believed UFOs and fairies inhabit the mountain, and space life resides in caverns inside the mountain. Passersby, hikers, and campers have heard machinery running and human moaning emerge from the hollows. There is conjecture by locals that creatures with a third eye, dressed in robes, have floated out of the mountains. It has been speculated that the inside of the mountain is a possible UFO base. It serves as a fuel pump to them, as the energy from volcanic activity is high. The aliens are drawn to those setups because it meets their needs for survival on Earth.

In regards to fairy sightings on Mount Shasta, I have personally heard slightly varying versions of the next story. A female camper, visiting Mount Shasta, sighted fairies. She witnessed a group of them together, hovering over plant life. Then, they all quickly buzzed away. (Sounds like trooping fairies to me.) These beings had insectlike wings and were only a few inches tall. That does fit the bill of the diminutive flower fairy. Amazing! I need to visit Mount Shasta!

Similarities between Fairies and UFOs

There is speculation that there are certain parallels between the fairy and the UFO. The comparisons are thought-provoking. Judge for yourself!

- Fairies and extraterrestrials are highly intelligent.
- Both are connected to leaving circles or rings on the ground.
- The two originate from a different dimension but may coexist with humans in this plane.
- Each prefers to remain undercover or invisible and to watch us and only appear when they wish to be seen.
- Both are deemed magical and smaller than humans.

The alien and the fairy both have the reputation as kidnappers. Recall that the changeling tale involves the fairy exchanging her own baby for a human one. The space inhabitant also practices abduction, typically women or children, in an effort to study them.

Both use the mystical Mount Shasta as a base since its volcanoes contain the necessary energy for both UFOs and fairies to recharge. These volcanoes act as gas stations for these entities.

If you have not had a true fairy experience or sighting, don't despair. Even though it may not be apparent, simple things, such as seeing a fairy ring made of toadstools, mushrooms, or flowers, is one telltale sign. Be on the lookout for other signs, such as rainbows, a sudden joyous feeling out of the blue, music in the distance, or shimmery light. If you are accepting, you will be the receiver of one or more telltale signs.

The next time you notice a flash or a flitting motion, grab your camera quickly. If on the prowl, or planning to visit any of the sites mentioned above, keep your camera handy. If you're feeling artistic, draft a sketch from memory while the image is still fresh. You may be our very next and best eyewitness.

It is a wonderful thing that people from different cultures all over the globe have witnessed fairies and are happy and willing to share their experiences.

When people stargazing, they stare at stars,
and many other things which they've already
presumed commonly and universally as stars.

—Toba Beta
Betelgeuse Incident: Insiden Bait Al-Jauza

Chapter 9

ARE YOU A FAIRY BELIEVER?

We call them faerie. We don't believe in them. Our loss.

—Charles de Lint

In 2016 I decided to conduct a survey on the number of people who believe in fairies. What was my motivation? After I completed my first book, *Passport to Heaven's Angelic Messages*, I wanted to present the subject of fairies to readers. As I mentioned this to others, the overall response I received was similar. People asked me, "Aren't fairies and angels the same thing? I really don't know the difference. I believe in angels but not in fairies." That was when I felt compelled to take a poll and hoped I would find a few fairy believers outside my spiritual circle.

Poll Demographics

My survey group consisted of fifty people in total—twenty-five males and twenty-five females, ranging in age from seventeen to eighty-eight. The annual income ranged from a student earning zero dollars to an individual earning $160,000 annually. The education level of the participants ranged from high school to a PhD.

Questions Posed

The fifty participants were asked to answer yes or no to the following questions:

1. Do you believe in angels?
2. Do you believe in fairies?
3. Do you believe in neither?
4. Are you unsure?

Interestingly, the responses were as follows:

Categories	Male	Female
Believes in angels	23	24
Believes in fairies	0	0
Believes in neither	2	1
Unsure	0	0

In my experience, men and women usually don't share similar views, but they did have much in common in this poll. Males and females answered in similar numbers to believing in the angels and not in the fairies.

From this sampling, there is a defininte awareness of angels, and that is fantastic news, but it's not such a favorable news bulletin for our fairy friends. Let's take a moment today and spread the joy of the fairy to one another!

You may be wondering how to know if a being is an angel or a fairy. Consider the following nine differences:

1. Angels are mentioned in the New International Version of the Bible 273 times, according to Christianity expert, Mary Fairchild (2011). It is up for debate whether fairies are revealed in the Bible. It is not as clear-cut as with the revelations about the angels. Mystical creatures like the unicorn and the dragon are mentioned in the King James Version of the Bible. According

to the website G<u>od Didn't Say That</u> (2017), "The [King James] translation refers to unicorns nine times and dragons over 30 times."

2. Angels are sources of light and power from God. They are pure and do not have egos or feelings like humans. Fairies and humans both express low-level emotions. Jealousy is one example. Remember Tinker Bell? She expressed envy.

3. Both angels and fairies may demonstrate light when present, but the light they emit is different. Angel light is white or pastel in color, while fairy light is bolder, like a happy string of party lights. Angel light is brighter, shimmery, and doesn't remain as long as fairy light. Fairy light is much dimmer.

4. The energy of the angel and fairy is different. Fairies move in a haphazard fashion. They are jumpy and hop from place to place. Angel energy moves in a straight line.

5. The wings of an angel are considered featherlike. The fairy has dragonfly-like wings.

6. Angels are presented in human proportions, whereas the fairy is a much smaller being.

7. The angel has relatively neat and long hair. The fairy's hair is tousled, loose, and sometimes kept in a short "pixie" style.

8. Angels sport halos. Certain categories of fairies sport wands.

9. Fairies can be found in nature, such as the forest, woods, farmland, trees, gardens, indoor plants, and near pets. Angels may be found anywhere. Some angels—for instance, the archangel Michael—have the ability to be in more than one place at the same time; fairies do not.

Some people do not believe in fairies, and some do. Everyone is entitled to his or her opinion and beliefs. I am very open to the possibly of that which we cannot always see. I am not just a believer in angels and fairies but also in ghosts, UFOs, Bigfoot, and the Jersey Devil (a legendary creature said to inhabit the Pine Barrens of southern New Jersey).

The believers in this world actually support a better scenario for society as a whole. Fairy lovers understand the importance of environmental care and the ramifications of not caring properly for the environment, which may have damaging effects on fairies and humans alike. Some people feel that fairy lovers are more compassionate, gentler people who more often have easygoing personalities. In my experience, that can be said for anyone who trusts in the unknown—angels, ghosts, and other supernatural activity.

If the critics are right that I've made all my decisions based on polls, then I must not be very good at reading them.

—Barack Obama

Fairy Delight
Popcorn drizzled with chocolate and sprinkles.

Fairy Star Wands
Fashion the stars from sugar cookie dough, bake,
decorate, harden, and place on stick.

Fairy Cloud Wands
These were created with marshmallows dipped in chocolate and sugar sprinkles.

Fairy Pretzel Wands
Dip pretzel sticks in chocolate and sugar sprinkles.

Fairy Grape Wands
Place the grapes on a lollipop stick.

My fairy wand display.

Fairy Liquid Refreshment
Choose any drink and dress it fairy-style.

Fairy cake
Too pretty to eat! Yet, I did. It was delicious.

Fairy Bites
Small muffins baked with multi-colored sprinkles mixed into the batter.

Fairy Bread Delight
Cut white bread into triangles, spread on a thin layer of
butter, and place colored sugar or sprinkles on top.

Fairy Lily Pads
Place frosting on sugar cookies and add sprinkles.

Fairy Parfaits
Prepared with set gelatin, cake, whipped cream, and magic sugar sparkles.

An example of a "fairy feast" created for children and adults.

Fairy Feast 2

Fairy Feast 3

My niece, Rowena, sporting a unicorn wig.

Rowena's hair fashioned into a unicorn horn.

The fairy residence I built for a fairy family.

These gigantic mushrooms appeared while I was writing
this fairy book. Tiny glitter orbs appeared near one of the
mushrooms after it was developed. Magical!

An up-close shot of the largest mushroom. Plenty
of tiny fairies could reside under it!

Toni Klein

The "Pop-Pop" butterfly. (Refer to Matt S' story in Appendix 3.)

My fairy dog statue creation.

My passionate football player son, Ian. Ian has always been
a very a good saver. I'm guessing he may still have the
money the tooth fairy gave to him so long ago!

Ian and me after one of his football games.

My lovely fairy caricature.
Courtesy of Barbara Thornton.

Chapter 10

FAIRY ENTERTAINMENT AND AMUSEMENT

The land of the fairy, where nobody gets old and godly
and grave, where nobody gets old and crafty and wise,
where nobody gets old and bitter of tongue.

—W. B. Yeats

Fairy-time fun is magical, sweet, and enjoyable. There are a multitude of delightful activities for indoors or the outdoor terrain to keep anyone, regardless of age, occupied for days! This chapter provides ideas aplenty and promises you will find at least one, most likely more, if you dare to try. The majority of the suggestions presented may be accomplished at a reasonable cost.

What fun is in store! Get ready to learn about fairy excursions in the USA and Ireland, creating fairy food, designing fairy rings and enchanting gardens, crafting fairy dust, learning the significance of fairy colors, and otherwise engaging in various fairy activities.

Fairy Excursions

DuPont Family Estate, Delaware

The DuPont family estate, built in 1907, is a historic country mansion once owned by Alfred I. DuPont and his wife. Located in Wilmington, Delaware, in what is known as "Chateau Country," it was opened to the public in 1951. The house and the Winterthur Museum have gorgeous gardens that are available for daily tours. A three-acre section of Winterthur was constructed specifically for children and the belief in fairies, magic, and fairy tales. Winterthur boasts a magical fairyland named the Enchanted Woods. It's said that fairies have taken up residence within these specially created woods. This garden is a true pleasure, especially for children but also for adults.

As I was writing *Fairies*, my husband and I took a very special trip to Delaware to celebrate our wedding anniversary. We visited the mansion, the grounds, and especially the expansive Enchanted Woods within Winterthur. Winterthur is captivating. Its features include a cottage, a troll bridge, a frog hollow, and a stone path. If you are in the area, do not miss the opportunity of visiting this unique estate and grounds. Antiques, vintage automobiles, and stunning gardens also await you and promise a pleasurable day.

Ireland

According to "A Guide to Finding Fairies: 15 Magical Places in Ireland," by Sadhbh Devlin (2015) on the blog Where Wishes Come From, Ireland offers mysterious fairy fascination to all, natives and visitors alike. Devlin's list of fifteen magical places is the ticket for those who live in or plan on visiting Ireland and want to combine the love of fairy haunts with a very pleasant day out with the family. Fairies are hanging out in beautiful parks and woods, which are filled with amazing fairy trails, trees equipped with fairy doors, and tiny residences, all filled with fairy wonder. This is on my bucket list, but in the meantime, I decided to conduct an internet expedition and visit via cyberspace. Each appears to host delightful parks, establishments, and truly gorgeous landmarks. The following is based on Ms. Devlin's information combined with my internet search of each site. Each is truly fascinating in its own way.

Northern Ireland
Mossley Mill, Belfast

In Mossley Mill, one should have no problem feeling the presence of fairies amid its ten-house fairy village with trails. It seems like the true feeling of what is imagined as fairy existence.

Dunshaughlin, County Meath
Rathbeggan Lakes Fairy Garden

This family-oriented garden offers fairy trees with magical doors. It is suggested to bring a ribbon along so that a wish can be made while fastening the ribbon to one of the fairy trees. I'm game!

Belvedere House
Mullingar, County Westmeath

As we realize, fairies are truly private beings. They reside at the Belvedere House but are very secretive and don't flaunt their whereabouts. At any rate, it appears to be a worthwhile jaunt, as it appears to be truly magical.

Corkagh Park Fairy Trail
Clondalkin, Dublin 22

This is a park is equipped for fun! Some activities include a petting farm (remember that fairies adore animals) and a play area (another beloved fairy activity). Fairies abound!

The Lullymore Fairies
Rathangan, County Kildare

This appears to be a special place to take the kiddies. According to Ms. Devlin, the park "embraced the folklore behind the lone Hawthorn tree that was there long before the park became 'a park' and how respectful they are of the fairy village that has grown around it."

Tymon Park Fairy Trail
Tallaght, Dublin 24

This outdoor expanse offers an awesome fairy trail which is thick with magical fairies. Bring along raisins to leave for the fairies along the trail as a treat. This promises to be a fun day outdoors.

The Marlay Park Fairy Tree
Rathfarnham, Dublin 16

This area provides a park with fairy landmarks that children will especially enjoy. It's said sometimes a washline may be spotted with tiny fairy apparel hanging on it.

Wells House Enchanted Woodland
Ballyedmond, County Wexford

Ms. Devlin highly endorsed this spot for parents and children to enjoy. A walk through the woods allows you to spy on many fairy doors on its trees.

The Fairy Trail
Union Hall, County Cork

It is suggested that you offer the fairies a few gifts when visiting this site. Keep in mind that fairies enjoy glistening crystals, polished rocks, chocolate and fruit. Therefore, if you decide to walk on this trail, you will be well prepared.

Derrynane House, Caherdaniel, County Kerry
Parknasilla Resort, Derryquin, County Kerry

Together these two sites are said to have unique fairy architecture. Derrynane House is a public museum, rich in folklore, and offers walking trails.

Fairy Mountain
Athea, Limerick

Fairy Mountain has a trail that sounds like a must-see because one particular tree may dissolve all of your worries by placing your hands in its trunk. (I may just catch a flight to Limerick tonight.)

Adare Manor Fairy Trail
Adare, Limerick

This spectacular manor offers a fairy trail with mini-fairy houses along the way. It's a great hideaway for the fairy with exceptional taste.

Templemore Park Fairy Trail
Templemore, County Tipperary

This is a very scenic park that includes a stone bridge, fairy doors on the trees, walking trails, and picnic areas. I'd bring a camera along to capture that magical moment.

Brigit's Garden
Roscahill, County Galway

Brigit's Garden is in western Ireland. A family-friendly award-winner, it is steeped in Celtic tradition. It comprises eleven acres of woods, gardens, meadows, a visitor center, cafe, gift shop, and a fairy fort. You may even host a special celebration, wedding, or birthday party there. It sounds like a fun and educational stop.

Fairy Food

Traveling is one love of my life, but food is probably higher up on the list. The kitchen is the perfect forum to create magical fairy treats. Certain fairies inhabit the kitchen and are known to love sweets. Chocolate and wrapped candies are very dear to them, yet fairies do believe in healthy foods too, like nuts.

Fairy food does not need to be pricey or difficult to make. Itemized below are simple and cost-effective ideas for hosting a child's party, and goodies to send to class on a birthday, to offer as a small gift, or just for pleasure and consumption.

Let's begin with my favorite—sweets. There are a few edible fairy wands—the cookie star, the marshmallow, and the pretzel wands.

The Cookie Star Wand

Items required:

- Sugar cookie dough
- Star-shaped cookie cutter
- Sugar sprinkles
- Lollipop sticks
- Flat pan
- Wax paper

First, flatten the dough. Next, use the cutter to make stars. Bake on a cookie sheet for best results. Immediately after the cookies are pulled from the oven, decorate them with sprinkles and slide the lollipop stick into the cookie. Be careful since the cookies will be hot. Place on waxpaper to set. You may also choose to "bling" the stick with pastel-colored sugar or pretty ribbons. Oo-la-la.

The Marshmallow Wand

Items required:

- Marshmallows
- Chocolate melts
- Edible sprinkles
- Lollipop sticks
- Holder to place the sticks upright

Place lollipop sticks in the marshmallows; then melt the chocolate. Dip and roll the marshmallows into the melted chocolate. Drizzle the sprinkles on them before the chocolate hardens. Place in the holder, and wait for the chocolate to set. This holder may be a homemade cardboard box with holes. The color of the chocolate is a personal preference. I like to dip mine in white or pink chocolate.

The Pretzel Wand

Items required:

- Pretzel sticks (use in place of a lollipop stick)
- Chocolate melts
- Sprinkles, cookie or chocolate chips
- Holder to place the wands upright

Melt the chocolate. Dip the pretzel stick. Before the chocolate hardens, adorn with sprinkles or small chocolate cookie chips or chocolate candies. Place in a holder until the choclolate hardens.

The Grape Wand

Items required:

- Grapes
- Lollipop sticks

This is super-easy and nutritious. Slide one grape after another grape onto the stick leaving enough room to hold it. Voila.

Miscellaneous Fairy Treats

Fairy Cubes

Items required:

- Colorful, fruity drink
- Ice cube tray

Pour the fruity drink into an ice cube tray. This may be a traditional square, crescents, stars, or other unique design. Various juice colors may be used to add dimensionality. Place in freezer. When frozen, the pretty ice cubes may be placed in a special fairy bowl or used in punch.

Fairy Punch

Items required:

- Homemade punch
- Sherbet
- Fairy cubes (see recipe above)
- Pretty punch bowl and ladle

It's best to choose your own recipe for the punch, as some children may have allergies. I make fairy punch from either pink lemonade or pink ginger ale. Ensure it is colorful and appealing. Pour it in the punch bowl, and add bright hues of sherbet and the ice cubes. (I feel like making some right now.)

Fairy Sandwiches

Items required:

- Bread
- Butter
- Sugar sprinkles

Cut the bread into triangles. Spread butter on each triangle, and decorate with sugar sprinkles.

Fairy Wraps

Suggested items:

- Cucumbers
- Nuts
- Large lettuce leaves
- Salad dressing (optional)

These wraps are more suitable for the adult pallet. If you're having a children's get-together with adults present, create these! Fairy wraps may be made by rolling either nuts or cucumbers in a large lettuce leaf. Drizzle with a tasty dressing (optional).

Fairy Delight

Items required:

- Popcorn (popped)
- Sugar glitter sprinkles
- Chocolate melts
- Flat pan
- Wax paper

Melt the chocolate. Dip the popcorn in melted chocolate. Place on the pan. Sprinkle sugar glitter on top of the dipped popcorn while the chocolate is still soft. Various chocolate color choices are available at most craft stores. I love to use white or pink bags of chocolates.

Pixy Stix—powdered candy that's packaged in a drinking straw–like paper stick—are a fairy delight. You can find Pixy Stix almost anywhere candy is sold.

There is pure merriment in hosting a party with your favorite fairy foods. (Refer to the photo section of this book for my fairy food creations.)

Outdoor Fairy Designs

Plenty of ways exist to celebrate our magical friends in nonedible ways as well. Let's move from the kitchen to the outdoors.

Designing a Fairy Ring

The fairy ring is a positive spot used to connect with fairies without distractions or to reflect, dream, meditate, or set your creative thoughts on fire. In folklore, fairy rings often were scary places where humans would disappear. Folklore warns not to fall asleep in a fairy ring or play or dance inside one. A fairy may bewitch the human and transport his or her mind to fairyland while the physical body remains behind, confused and dazed.

As a precaution, respect the ring. It is not advisable to step within the circle, destroy it, or let another mock it. According to legend, fairy rings left untouched and enjoyed for their beauty will attract good fortune. Invite the fairies into a ring. Do not invade the space. Enjoy the aesthetic appeal, and it will bring you good luck.

The flower ring is an area where the fairies gather to folic, especially during dawn and dusk. It is commonly a nature-made grassy mound or circle of wild mushrooms or field-grown flowers. However, a fairy ring may be man-made as well. The design and set-up of a fairy ring is fairly easy. Individuals interested in attracting fairies to their property or like the look tend to create these. Two tranquil ways to create personal lawn fairy rings is to use flowers or rocks. Decide on the size of the ring you prefer; then decorate it with your desired outline. If a shiny stone or coin is placed in the center of the circle, the fairies quickly spot your specially designed ring and come inside.

The flower ring may be adorned with the fairy's favorite flower. You may attract them by using any of the following:

- Sunflowers
- Honeysuckle
- Daisies
- Rosemary and thyme
- Lavender
- Heliotrope
- Foxglove
- Lily of the valley
- Snowdrops
- Primrose
- Solomon's seal
- Ferns
- Bluebells
- Yellow archangel

Additionally, ornamental grasses dotted here and there adds a nice touch.

Some friendly fairy advice is to stay clear of the following choices, as these are turn-offs to the fairy:

- Herbs (not including rosemary and thyme)
- St. John's wort
- Red verbena
- Rowan (mountain ash)
- Four-leaf clover

Let's get started.

1. Select an area in your yard for the fairy ring.
2. Dig a small ditch on the perimeter for an assortment of colorful plants.
3. Position the plants. The fairies will guide you as your garden assumes its own artform.

You may continue decorating your ring with sparkly ornaments, which will make the area more attractive to fairies. If you wish to visit the fairy ring at dusk or dawn, when it is especially active with fairies, feel free to place lanterns or solar lights in the area.

Rock Ring

The rock ring may be small or large in diameter. Because the fairies are diminutive, it doesn't need to be large. Use natural stones or genuine gemstones for your rock ring, rather than man-made rocks. Natural stones that have been polished are acceptable. These may be purchased with words imprinted on them (for example, love, harmony, peace). Since the fairy adores anything that gleams or glitters, an authentic stone that is painted with metallic colors is very appealing. It's your circle too, so choose stones that make you happy to gaze upon and that you enjoy. For instance, I like to paint my rocks a mixture of silver and gold. Also, I use eleven rocks for my circles, as that's the number of my birth month, November. The rock circle is especially fun to create with a child.

Always be on the lookout for a naturally made fairy ring. You might have a ring on your property already, fashioned by the fairies themselves. A fairy-made ring most commonly will be a circle of mushrooms. If you see this, please do not disturb it. The mushrooms act as shelter from the elements to these tiny beings, and they do not appreciate others tampering with their homes (just as we humans don't either). It is imperative to demonstrate respect for their sacred zone, and it is bad karma to meddle with a fairy ring.

Whether space is abundant or limited, homemade fairy rings are possible for all. It can even be a circle of small stones on a tiny spot of grass. Be inventive and let your creative juices flow.

Enchanted Gardens

Enchanted gardens are those situated outside or inside (as miniatures). The space in your yard dedicated as the fairy garden may be adorned with the special plants, fairy statuary, and any shiny, shimmery object. Coins, polished rocks, shells, and beach glass do the trick. A small waterfall, fountain or small pond is a nice enhancement since fairies are attracted to the water.

According to the website Fairy Gardening (2017), the concept of the fairy garden first made its appearance in the United States—a bonsai-style miniature garden—at the World's Fair in Chicago in 1893. Later, the *New York Times* featured an article on this type of small garden. (Once a good idea hits New York City, it becomes the rage for the rest of the country.) Over 120 years later, that first fairy garden has morphed into so much more, which so many people love.

If a wooded area is part of your property, you may wish to design a fairy forest trail, laid with wood chips, fairy signs, and hanging prisms, as well as fairy doors on a few trees. This may act as a private refuge for your family, pets, and the fairies. If you live in an urban area, don't despair. You still may create several fantastic fairy touches to adorn your abode, such as the following:

- Hang crystals or colorful ribbons on trees.
- Post lawn signs. These are available with fanciful fairy images or clever sayings. You can find a variety of wooden signs on websites like eBay, Pinterest, or Etsy. (A word of caution: Photos can be deceiving. Check the dimensions of the sign before you buy, as some are for miniature gardens, and others are large yard signs.)

- Hang wind chimes, which not only are decorative but offer a pretty melody and summon the fairies.
- Decorate a tree with a fairy door. I also have placed a miniature fence leading to the door and planted flowers alongside it.
- Purchase a "tree face" kit—these are eyes, a nose, and a mouth that are placed on the tree so it appears to have a face. It's a cute touch.

When I was a little girl, my grandmother said that fairies mark their visit to the garden, ring, or other specially created place by leaving a small gift. This gift may arrive in the form of a gorgeous sunset, a magnificent feather, or a tiny twist of wind that blows harmlessly through the dirt. This demonstrates the fairies are happy with our efforts in creating a special place for them. The next time you witness one of these nature surprises, remember that it might have been from one of your fairy companions.

Indoor Fairy Activities

If you prefer to stay indoors and still make a fairy connection, I have indoor fairy activities just for you.

Glitter Pens

Pretty glitter pens are a good way for a child to create personalized fairy notes, stationery, or artwork. (I am just gaga over glitter pens.) These pens may serve as a reward for a child's good grades or exemplary behavior.

Bottles

Bottle-making is another great activity. It requires only a bottle or mason jar. Paint the glass, or fill the bottle or jar with pretty lights or fairy figurines. The possibilities are as limitless as your imagination.

The Flower Crown

Items required:

- Floral wire
- Wire cutters
- Clear tape
- Flowers

These crowns are quite the rage these days for all ages and are fairly easy to construct. This type of headband is ideal for a youngster, teenager, bridesmaid, as a gift, or an added accessory to a favorite outfit. Flower crowns may be fashioned from real or artificial flowers. Fashion your crown by first twisting and cuttting the wire to the desired fit around your head. Next, attach the flowers to the wire with the tape and create. Have fun!

Clothespin Fairies

Items required:

- Glue or glue gun
- Clothespins
- Material for its dress and wings (felt, paper or fabric)
- Acrylic paint
- Pipe cleaners
- Ribbon
- Stickers (optional)

Little girls (and I) love these! I shop at the dollar store for the bulk of my supplies. Here are the steps:

1. Cut a hole in the fabric and place over the ball at the top of the clothespin.
2. Tie the ribbon into a bow around the "waist."
3. Attach your handmade wings with a pipe cleaner or glue.

4. Paint on the face, and let it dry completely. Stickers may be used on the face.

You have just brought a little fairy into the world!

Interior Decorating

Several rooms in the home lend themselves to fairy accompaniments. My sunporch is decorated fairy-style. I have added special plants, an indoor fairy garden, fairy statues, purple and pink party lights, and small figurines. It all flows very nicely. It is a pleasant room, with the sun streaming in and the presence of the tiny beings it attracts.

Decals

Decals are a lovely extra touch to place on a child's bedroom wall, playroom, or on a car window. They are relatively inexpensive, easy to affix, and contribute a personal and pleasing look to the space.

Bumper Stickers and Magnets

These are charming tribute to the enchanting beings. Place a bumper sticker or magnet on the refrigerator, car, garden gate, or anywhere your heart desires.

Indoor Garden

Create a little garden in a special pot with flowers, plants, mini-signs, and fairy furniture. Set the pot in any location where a little magic is desired.

Crafting Fairy Dust

Fairy dust or pixie dust is much more than an aesthetic pleasure; it is a staple item in fairyland. Fairy dust has valuable mystical importance. It not only helps with wish-making but offers protection to us humans.

Use it to adorn an item, like jewelry. It may be given as a magical gift, and some people state it helps nurture plants and crops if a drop is placed into the soil.

Fairy dust may be store-bought or homemade. Many colors are available at the art supply store. Some varieties even have glitter mixed throughout.

There are various recipes for creating homemade fairy dust. I will share both the nonedible and edible varieties.

Nonedible Fairy Dust

Creating nonedible fairy dust is a two-step process that's a blast!

Items required:

- Salt, a nontoxic powder, or finely crushed chalk
- Glitter (Any glitter will work, but super-fine glitter makes the best fairy dust.)

1. Mix the two items together. A two-to-one powder-to-glitter ratio is best, but it's your personal choice.
2. Store in an airtight container.

Caution: When handling fairy dust, always be *very careful* to keep it away from your eyes—make this clear to children as well. Also impress on children that the dust is not edible, so they should not put it in their mouths.

One of my favorite fairy activities is designing and filling small decorative bottles with the dust. It is best to use a funnel with a small hole to avoid spillage. (Please refer to my examples of personally designed fairy bottles in the photo section.)

Edible Fairy Dust

Making edible fairy dust has its own advantages.

Items required:

- Sugar
- Confectioner's sugar
- Food coloring
- Cookie sheet

1. Blend sugar and confectioner's sugar together. (Experiment with your own consistency.)
2. Add a drop or two of food coloring. (Too many drops will result in clumps.)
3. Spread on a cookie sheet.
4. Let stand for a half hour, or bake for a few minutes at 350 degrees. Use care not to overcook your dust.

If you're using more than one color, it's best to bake each color separately.

Feel free to scatter your edible dust onto cakes, cupcakes, cereal, cookies, ice cream, and other foods. A degree of enchantment is certainly added when entertaining with this personalized product.

Fairy dust is a fun way to add magic to any occasion—parties, gift giving, or when entertaining a child. A fun idea for children is to assist them sprinkle the dust outdoors while he or she whispers a message to the fairies. It is also nice for adults to scatter dust on stationary for that friend who loves bling, or to make special items with the colorful dust as presents. Some people even request a spiritual member of the community or a person certified in Reiki to bless it. This ensures extra blessings and benefits, especially when giving the fairy dust as a gift.

The Significance of Fairy Colors

The color of fairy dust has significance and meaning. I craft my bottles depending on the color's significance. For example, if I am creating a gift for a friend who is looking to land a great new job, I may select green dust and attach a thoughtful message to the bottle.

When selecting colors for your crafts, consider the following meanings of each color:

- Black: secrecy, power, stability
- Blue: trust, truth, peace
- Gold: wisdom, success, confidence
- Green: success, prosperity
- Orange: excitement, playfulness, harmony
- Pink: love, romance, attraction, affection
- Purple: ambition, imagination, persuasiveness
- Red: power, energy, desire
- Rose: friendship, honesty, reliability
- Violet: imagination, strength, ambition
- White: protection, innocence, purity
- Yellow: joy, happiness, optimism, creativity

Time to get started! Many magical, memorable, and fun-filled hours await in crafting fairy rings, fairy-dust bottles, gardens, and much more. Perhaps you are already proficient in designing fairy crafts and wish to turn your talent into a sideline business. Whatever the motivation, fairy crafts produce a happy atmosphere in the home for you, your family, and your visitors. Ignite your creative juices, feel the inspiration, and, most of all, have fun!

In the fairy stories, naming is knowledge. When I know your name, I can call your name, and when I call your name, you'll come to me.

—Jeanette Winterson

Chapter 11

MY PERSONAL FANCIFUL POETRY COLLECTION

The fairy poet takes a sheet
Of moonbeam, silver white;
His ink is dew from daisies sweet,
His pen a point of light.

—Joyce Kilmer

Poetry may be seen as a delicate form of writing geared toward a certain topic. I first began writing fanciful fairy poetry so I could place the verse on the handcrafted fairy bottles I designed. Each bottle I created had a different purpose. Some appealed to the fairies for love and some for career or other various petitions.

I added sparkly items to the fairy bottles, along with my poetry. My original plan was to make these as gifts with mystical poetry for special occasions and present them to special people in my life. Later, a friend suggested I sell my pretty bottles for others' enjoyment. Please feel free to use my poems on greeting cards, your own crafts, or other well-wishing pieces.

My fairy poetry eventually evolved into angel poetry and poetry prayers, which I've also included in this chapter. You may have an angel lover or prayer warrior in your life who will find these useful. I hope you enjoy them and can use it in your own way.

I feel poetry brings a certain amount of calmness to life. Believe in the beyond to help you in the areas of love, success, career, personal power, and riches. Feel free to chant these poems as an affirmation of an already realized prayer or wish for your life.

Fairy Poetry

The Fairy of Love

I hold for you this bottle of special love dust.
Imagine it move about, and watch as it pours.
Then concentrate on your true love
and this love will be yours!
***

The Fairy of Success

Each day blessings are wished
your way in order for you
to reach your goals and
accomplishments; enjoy freedom and
all your heart's desires!
***

The Career Fairy

Allow this fairy dust
to carry you away
to a special job opportunity
with great pay!
***

The Personal Power Fairy

A powerful being;
That is what you are.
You shed light on others, near and far.
Never forget you can do what you set your mind to,
And because of your goodness
Everyone will cherish you!

***

The Fairy of Riches

The fairy says to visualize money
coming your way each day.
If you do, a gain
should float your way!

***

Angel Poetry

The following breezy angel poetry is dedicated to the important people
in your life: mothers, grandmothers, daughters, sisters, aunts, nieces,
cousins, friends and even your hairstylist. Dedicate these poems to
those special beings in your life when you want to share with them how
you feel.

Mother

Mother, I send to you this special
angel's light to protect,
guide, and remind you of
my deep love.
Keep the special angels near,
and think of me while you receive
all the wonderful
blessings sent to you from above.

Thank you for being
a wonderful mother.
To me, there could
be no other!
I love you!
***

Grandmother

Grandmother,
this angel prayer is
sent from heaven just for you.
May the angels protect and guide you in all you do.
I love you!
***

Daughter

Daughter,
you are my daughter and my friend.
Our circle of love will never end.
The bond we share
is a special love.
And I send to you
happy blessings from above!
***

Sister

Sister,
may this special angel wish
surround you with
protection and happiness.
I send you sweet thoughts to remind you of
our special friendship and love.

I wish you bountiful
blessings from above!
***

Aunt

Aunt,
it is nice to know I was blessed
with you as my aunt
and can count on you
each and every day
May the light of the angels
protect you and send love
and happiness your way.
Keep the angels and me close to you.
heart in all you do.
Always remember how much
I love you!
***

Niece

Niece, you are such a
special person,
and I wanted
you to know.
I send angel's dust
to offer happiness
and light, which will
make your life glow.
Keep it close as a
special keepsake, and think
of a wish you'd like to make.
***

Cousin

Cousin,
you are my special cousin,
my family,
my friend.
I think of you
fondly every day,
so this magical angel wish is a gift I send to you.
May it provide happiness and blessings in all you do!
***

Friend

Friend,
I sent special and angelic light
and protection to
you my dear friend.
May the angels offer
you hope, protection, love
and guidance every day!
May you also remember me fondly
in every way.
***

Hairstylist

To my hairstylist:
You are my precious stylist.
This is true.
No one could ever replace you.
I come in looking not my best.
You always make me beautiful and
put my fears to rest!
***

Prayerful Poetry

Prayers may be said in traditional and nontraditional ways. I've included various poetry prayers as suggestions to be recited for specific areas in your life. The following prayers may assist you in new ways to express thanks or ask for heavenly help in areas such as a love dilemma or other life quandaries.

Thank You (Prayer One)

Thank you to the Creator and his heavenly beings.
I know you watch over us and guard our feelings.
It is so incredible how you demonstrate your power.
To the word you and your angels ever so shower.

***

Thank You (Prayer Two)

The angels, fairies, moon, and stars are the Lord's beautiful creations.
To you, God, I offer a standing ovation.
Thank you for all the goodness and love I receive.
I greatly appreciate it and know in my heart
this feeling will never leave.

***

Love Assistance

Angels of love, please bring the perfect love into my life.
This relationship cannot be filled with grief and strife.
Please help the one for my highest good to enter my life immediately.
I would appreciate your help, which I seek so desperately.

Or you may substitute the last two lines:
Please help the one for my highest good to enter my life without delay.
I would appreciate your help in every way.

***

Financial Assistance

God and his heavenly helpers, I implore you to
help me with my financial situation today.
I have so many debts and obligations I must pay.
Please, I pray for the arrival of relief from a happy, positive source.
So that I may never again be filled with dread and remorse.

***

Career-Seeking Prayer

Angels and fairies, help me in my job searchlight.
To find a private appointment would be a sweet delight.
Support and guide me to the primary place.
My gratefulness for your assistance I could never raise.

***

I hope you enjoyed these poems and found them useful. Perhaps I have
inspired the poet in you.

Life itself is a wonderful fairy tale.

—Hans Christian Andersen

Chapter 12

MYSTICAL-INSPIRED IDENTIFICATION

In the fairy stories, naming is knowledge. When I know your name, I can call your name, and when I call your name, you'll come to me.

—Jeanette Winterson

Fairy names are charming, delightful, and captivating. Recently many couples are popularizing fairy names by giving their newborn babies an enchanting moniker. Those who love the idea but don't plan to have children or who already have grown children opt to name their pets or even automobiles with a fairy name—even a mermaid or other magical being name—for luck!

Choosing a name is a very personal and well-thought-out choice for most people. Perhaps the offerings below may assist in that choice. These lovely female and stately male names are each a distinctive, unique choice.

Girls	Boys
Aerwyna	Alfred
Aine	Alvaro
Alvina	Brokk
Calypso	Clean
Dariyah	Drake
Elvina	Elvin
Fairy	Foster
Fay	Genius
Marigold	Kalen
Marin	Kellen
Muirgen	Oberon
Naida	Oren
Oops	Orin
Pixie	Puck
Radella	Rosevelt
Sen	Sindri
Tiana	Suelita
Zanna	Warren

Many mystical names exist. For more ideas, please refer to http://www.momjunction.com and http://www.fairiesworld.com.

I love to name my automobile because I do feel my car is my friend, and I become very attached to it. Even though it's a machine, the energy it exudes presents a feeling to me as if it possesses male or female energy. The last vehicle I owned presented a definite feminine vibe to me. I named her Naida. Naida is said to be a perfect and beautiful fairy in every way. I felt this was a fitting name for my stunning red car, hence she was named Naida. I even named my son's car Dominique for two reasons: (1) I feel it emanates feminine energy, and (2) my son, Ian's, mechanic's name is Dom.

If you feel the same way about autos, then you will understand this philosophy. Whether a kitten, doggie, fairy tree, or automobile, assigning a magical name is a lighthearted and fun activity. Give it a try. The winged beings are on board!

As you see, fairies can provide all kinds of creative outlets.

Fairies have to be one thing or the other, because being so small they unfortunately have room for one feeling only at a time.

—J. M. Barrie, *Peter Pan*

Author's Note

Thank you "fairy much" for selecting my book *Fairies*. It proves you are an individual who is open-minded and accepting and who has a diverse mind-set and is secure in his or her beliefs. You have no issue with having faith in things not visibly present to the naked eye. Although the scientific world may dispute the idea of fairies, we fairy supporters have the benefit of a life filled with marvel, magic, and surprise.

There are definite advantages to holding a belief of fairies. Those individuals who do are deemed creative and imaginative. The acceptance of fairies offers a level of comfort and escape from the drudgery of everyday life, and it opens us to new hobbies and pleasures, writings and movies, costumes, decorations, and hair art, just to name just a few. Due to these little beings, we are able to feed our imaginations and add lightheartedness to everyday life.

As for me, I do not dismiss the thought of any supernatural activities or beings that may be present and share our world. After all, who doesn't need a little magic in life from time to time.

I hope you enjoyed reading about the fairies and the other elementals as much as I have enjoyed writing about them.

Please feel free to contact me with any thoughts, feedback, or experiences at toniklein@ymail.com.

Check out my Facebook page at "Toni Klein Author."

I look forward to bringing you more books in the future.

Enjoy!

Appendix 1

THE MYSTERIOUS UNICORN
AND MERMAID

Toads are to dragons what carrots are to unicorns.

—Ness Kingsley, *The Curse of Cackling Meadows*

Mermaids and unicorns are visionary, exquisite, fascinating creatures. Each in its own way has added such beauty and mystery to the world. Are they real? Do they exist? You decide!

The Magical Unicorn

The renowned unicorn is visually similar to the horse except for its magical spiral horn embedded in its forehead. In folklore, the unicorn's horn was a valuable commodity—it was thought to cure diseases—and so the unicorn was hunted for its precious horn. Because of this, the unicorn became extinct. Other versions of folklore claim unicorns are no longer on this earth because Noah did not put any on the ark. Yet other tales say unicorns presently live on Earth but choose to remain invisible, as a self-protection tool.

In the days of the unicorn, young maidens were the only ones who could capture one, as these girls were the epitome of purity and innocence. Thousands of years ago, the unicorn was not what we envision today. Rather, it was much larger and not at all as dainty as today's depictions. It had huge feet and resembled a rhinoceros. Today the unicorn is portrayed as very pretty, graceful, and inspirational. When my son, Ian, was very young, if an adult discussed an unpleasant topic in his presence, he would say, "Puppies, unicorns." This was his way of adding happy thoughts to the conversation. To this day, if a chat takes an undesirable turn, I think about that cute statement, chuckle, and mentally recite to myself, *Puppies, unicorns.*

The King James Version of the Bible references the unicorn. Numbers 23:22 states, "God brought them out of Egypt; he hath as it were the strength of a unicorn." Some folks assert the unicorn was actually a rhino, but art from that period does illustrate a true unicorn. During your next museum visit, look for pieces of ancient unicorn artwork. Decide for yourself!

People are mystified by the unicorn. Unicorn lovers perform may activities to feel close to the mystical being and keep the idea alive. Some are outlined below:

Unicorn Costume

Don a special mystical get-up, and make your next Halloween event a smash! You will reflect a dreamlike presence.

Unicorn-Themed Party

Host a jubilant afternoon tea that is unicorn-themed, featuring unicorn-style cupcakes, cakes, and/or chocolate lollipops. Or feature the unicorn at a child's party. The hostess and attendants may be extravagant and entertain in a unicorn hat, other cute items, or full regalia. Decorate using streamers and twinkle lights, or hang a fairy-dust banner and use rainbow colors. This event would be extra pretty in the garden.

Unicorn Hair Braiding

Hair braiding, unicorn-style, is a new fad. It involves twisting and braiding the top section of the hair and fashioning it into a unicorn horn. Tutorials are available on the internet on how to construct a unicorn braid. Some people choose to add bright colors to the hair to enhance the overall look.

Unicorn Hairpiece

A multitude of pretty unicorn wigs and colored extensions are for sale. They are typically long and come in different styles and colors. Some even feature horns. My niece Rowena offered to fashion her hair into a unicorn braid hairstyle and to model a unicorn wig. Please refer to the photo gallery featured in middle portion of this book.

Unicorn Music

A musical group named the Irish Rovers sing about the unicorn. "The Unicorn Song" is very cute and available on YouTube. The Irish Rovers sing about why we don't see the unicorn today.

Unicorn Day

The unicorn has its own special day! National Unicorn Day falls on April 9! Celebrate this occasion by baking a unicorn cake, wearing a unicorn hair piece, or purchasing a unicorn item such as a keychain or stuffed toy. Today, many unicorn items are available such as decorations, baked goods, candy and more. Use your imagination and have a glorious day!

The unicorn is a highly precious creature. Although many regard it as pure fantasy, it has value in our society. Some people are adamant that the unicorn did exist at one point, but over time, this beautiful being became extinct. Perhaps today the unicorn does live on invisibly, deep in the forest, unseen, in an effort to protect itself. Perhaps one day it will reemerge, when the world is ready for it once again.

The Marvelous Mermaid

The ever-so-elusive mermaid is known across the land. Mermen, the male counterpart, coexist with mermaids. Mermen prefer to remain under the radar, whereas mermaids are more highly recognized in folklore sightings. Some folks are surprised mermen exist.

Mermaids sometimes are seen as dangerous, as shipwrecks and other hazardous events are connected to them. Folklore tells of many innocent men who have been were lured to their deaths by the mermaid or the siren, who are somewhat similar to the mermaid. Others see the mermaid as a happy and good creature.

Mermaids, are best described as having a human female body to the waist. The lower portion consists of fish scales and a fin. In Greek mythology, merpeople were considered messengers of the sea.

In British folklore, mermaids were often considered messengers of bad fortune, as they had the capability if creating horrendous sea storms, which could cause harm to or kill humans.

The mermaid is also legendary for luring a man into falling in love with her. The human male falls under her spell—some mermaids single out the mariner by hypnotizing him—and he is so very attracted to the mermaid that he can't help but leave the crew to marry her.

On occasion, mermaids may bring good fortune to us by granting wishes or providing cures to those with deathly illnesses.

The Cornish circulate tales of mermaids who are stunningly gorgeous. They often are seen combing their magnificent golden hair, and they never age.

Other countries believe that persons with psychic abilities are granted this gift only because a mermaid bestowed a special kindness.

I'd like to share a few curious tidbits. I learned of the first three tales when I was a small girl; a good friend who is a world traveler told me the fourth. As a child I was mesmerized by mermaids, and this still holds true today.

Are the following true encounters? You be the judge.

Many years ago, a young boy in a Scotland discovered a mermaid. She quickly trusted him, and they became close friends. It was a short-lived friendship, however, as the boy killed her. He never explained why. Villagers speculated that he fell in love with her, but she did not return the romantic love. The villagers felt so horrible for the mermaid that they provided her with an elaborate human burial.

Also many years ago, a man in a coastal town stumbled across a mermaid who had washed ashore. She was badly hurt, so he carried her to a nearby lake, placed her in the water, and tended to her injuries. The two fell in love and were married, and she healed. Could it have been a case of true love that really cured her? In this story, we don't know if she remained a mermaid or was transformed into a human being after her marriage. I rationalized that to survive on land, she would need to be a human. Either way, the couple was deliriously happy. Perhaps marriage and true love can be a transformer.

A group of seafaring men observed a number of gorgeous young women, swimming around the perimeter of the ship. The men could not help but call to them. Naturally very excited and curious, these men decided to dive into the sea and meet the girls. To their astonishment, they discovered the girls were half-human/half-fish creatures. The men felt a need to seize these beauties, but although they tried, the mermaids swam deeper and deeper underwater, leading the men to their deaths. Or was it really that they led the men to their underwater world?

More recently, a female was spotted off the coast of the Mediterranean Sea. She began fascinating boaters with her tricks. Witnesses claimed she was an actual mermaid, living in the area. The locals were so excited to hear this, as they felt it would boost tourism. A handsome reward was offered to anyone who could produce authentic photographs or other factual proof. Sadly, no one could obtain such evidence, and the hope of a real-life mermaid quickly evaporated.

I'm fascinated by stories of the supernatural. I have been almost hypnotized while listening. I never discount anything mysterious, unexplained, or magical!

Today, it is common for individuals to represent these charming creatures in their choice of jewelry, by hosting themed parties, by watching mermaid movies or attending plays, and by decorating both indoor and outdoor spaces with their splendor. Last year, my husband and I attended a local holiday-house tour. One particular home showcased a kitchen full of mermaid paraphernalia. It was very attractive. If you have a love of mermaids, there are numerous ways to enjoy them.

Mermaid Fun Facts

- Mermaids have long, beautiful hair and are known to comb it often. They adore gazing into a mirror at themselves while doing so.
- Mermaids not only live in the sea but also in rivers and lakes.
- It is ill advised to treat a mermaid unkindly. If so, the human will suffer immeasurably.
- Mermaids and merman coexist. The mermaid is spotted more frequently than her merman counterpart and is more recognized in folklore. Mermen are much larger creatures and, unlike the mermaids, do not have the interest in human life. Harbor towns or societies on the sea without a doubt carry more tales of the mermaid than the merman.
- In 1836, Hans Christian Andersen penned the fairy tale, *The Little Mermaid*. It was a brilliantly written story about a mermaid who wishes to marry a prince and live as a normal human girl with real legs. This desire doesn't quite work out in her favor. Could it be the moral is to never compromise yourself to gain that special someone into your life? There have been

many adaptations of *The Little Mermaid*. My husband and I enjoyed seeing the ballet in San Francisco a few years back. What a perfect evening that was. The mermaid has the power to enrapture us!

- Christopher Columbus, in his travel journal, reported spotting mermaids. He detailed exactly what he witnessed—finlike women who rose out of the sea to its surface. Columbus did not depict them they as the stunning-looking women as are in the old tales we hear today. It's very interesting that Columbus, a well-recognized explorer, saw mermaids too.

Mermaid lore is as ancient as the sea but still present in our society today. It is kept alive through children's stories and literature, in the modern adaption of *The Little Mermaid* film by Disney, in folklore, in artwork, and more. It is fun to imagine a secret world beneath the sea, where mermaids and mermen live together, isn't it? I have often envisioned what it would be like and have wanted to visit—but not remain there.

Unicorns and mermaids add to this world's wonder. I am grateful their stories are passed down through time and that the media keeps it alive. Perhaps one day, the unicorn will emerge and the mermaid will take a selfie, and we will have definite proof. Until then, I dare to dream.

> But what use is the unicorn to you if your
> intellect doesn't believe in it?
>
> —Umberto Eco

Appendix 2

THE SPIRITUAL BUTTERFLY

What the caterpillar calls the end of the
world, the master calls a butterfly.

—Richard Bach

The butterfly, a multicultural symbol loved by countless people, is a
life-form that holds divine qualities.

The butterfly has four stages of life. Each serves a different purpose
and takes on a totally different look. Its life begins as an egg, and then it
hatches into a caterpillar. Shedding its skin several times, it forms into
a cocoon, and eventually the beautiful butterfly emerges. Our lives are
reminiscent of the butterfly. For instance, the baby stages are points of
defenselessness, growth, learning, and eventual expansion developing
into a mature adult. This is the reason why the butterfly represents
transformation. Its metamorphosis is incredible. Yes, we humans and
the butterfly are alike. Ponder this: similar to the butterfly, we also are
on a journey in life and go through different cycles. We begin slowly
and explore the world, like the caterpillar. Later, we become like the
cocoon, only to later venture out and fly like the butterfly. Fortunately,
we have much longer life spans than the butterfly, who lives less than

one month. Butterflies remind us that even though we experience longer life spans, our lives flash right before our eyes. We are wise to cherish and love each moment. The butterfly teaches us to enjoy our freedom and not to take life too seriously.

In addition to transformation, the butterfly characterizes many things: joy, resurrection, the soul, spiritual growth, feminine energy, celebration, and elegance, just to name a few.

Butterflies are important in various cultures. In some societies, it forecasts a birth, a change in career, or a loved one's communication from heaven. No matter the reason, butterflies are beautiful symbolic couriers.

Fairies, angels and spirit guides may wish to connect with us through the butterfly. When the butterfly presents itself, it is a true signal. When a butterfly appears, it most likely indicates your guardian angel or spirit guide is sending you a signal. It is difficult to ignore a butterfly's presence, so consider it an important communicator.

Native Americans believe the butterfly represents joy, freedom, and creativity. Christians profess it's a symbol of resurrection and faith. As we experience transitions in our lives, we should keep the faith. The butterfly is a transitional figure that proves life gets better. Immortalized as a true symbol of the soul, butterflies are said to be engraved on ancient Christian tombs. Greek mythology links the butterfly with the soul.

Departed loved ones can speak to us through butterflies. Many people report seeing butterflies shortly after a loved one's death. This is quite comforting, as it is a message from beyond saying, "Hello. I'm okay. I'm here for you."

Butterflies may act as spirit guides. They tend to appear when a human needs help and validation that things will be okay. We may call upon it for help when we feel worried, lost, or need a change in life. Try enlisting the help of the butterfly.

The butterfly receives homage in exciting ways. A few examples include art, collectibles, Halloween costumes, decorative objects, garden ornaments, sending butterfly kisses, placing a butterfly bandage on a wound, and in songs. One popular song titled "Butterfly Kisses" was written by Bob Carlisle especially for his teenage daughter, Brooke. His initial intention was not to record it but to send a special message through song to her. This song was well received and won the 1997 Grammy Award for Best Country Song. I remember the song well, since my son, Ian, was born that year, and we would listen to the song together.

In art, the butterfly can be traced back to 1350 BC in Egypt. At that time, butterflies were depicted through paintings placed on tombs. During the Renaissance, butterflies also were found in art. In fact, they have moved up through time to modern day. The butterfly symbolizes the perfect art form, with its beauty, symmetrical form, and colors. Butterflies added to any artwork offer a fairy-tale–type quality. I am familiar with artists who add butterflies to their work to add a hint of femininity. Recently I was in a local gallery that showcased the most beautiful stained-glass mosaic work. The butterflies were protruding out of the frame, offering a three-dimensional look—gorgeous. (Purchasing that is on my bucket list.)

Even modern medicine recognizes the butterfly in one of its techniques—the butterfly bandage. This particular bandage's shape is like that of butterfly wings. It is used to seal small but deep wounds by holding the cut together so it does not gape. This promotes quicker healing and less scaring. In a sense, it's another miraculous contribution of the butterfly.

I just love a butterfly sandwich and have held special memories of these since my childhood. When I was six, my best friend's mother would surprise us with butterfly sandwiches. She would cut the sandwich in an X shape, that is, diagonally and then do the same again, resulting in four small triangles. She would then place the inner points together, forming two small sandwiches shaped as butterflies. My visits to my best friend's house became extra special.

There are superstitions about butterflies. If a butterfly is seen anywhere, it is an omen of good health. If one is seen in the house, it means an impending marriage. If someone pulls off a butterfly's wing, it is a bad omen. If one dreams of a butterfly, it denotes prosperity, good times, freedom, positivity, and a good life.

Witnessing the butterfly is always a lovely event. It suggests spiritual insight and reminds us of our own spiritual paths. Next time you see one, take a moment out of your busy day to stand in awe of it.

The butterfly counts not months but moments and has time enough.

—Rabindranath Tagore

Appendix 3

MAGICAL TRUE-LIFE
FAIRY EXPERIENCES

I'm an interpreter of stories. When I perform it's like
sitting down at my piano and telling fairy stories.

—Nat King Cole

It is truly amazing that the world contains magical moments, such as those described here. I am optimistic that as you read these adventures, you will feel a part of these true-life testimonials. The first three are my own experiences.

When I was eleven years old, I was visiting my father's parents one weekend. My grandparents lived in Harrington Park, New Jersey, which was about two hours away from our home in Allentown. That day I was sitting in my grandparents' living room when my grandmother, whom I called Mom, sat me down in a more serious manner than usual. She told me about the night she saw tiny fairy people. Mom said she chose to tell me of this story only because she knew I would believe her.

The week prior to our visit, she said, for three nights in a row, she awoke as dawn was breaking, and she noticed tiny people dancing in a circle in the garden. She told my grandfather, but he said she was dreaming. I did believe Mom. She was a serious German woman, and if she said she saw fairies, she certainly saw fairies!

* * *

My grandmother on my mother's side, whom I called Gram, lived in Ireland before she relocated to Hamilton, Scotland, when she was a youngster. She claimed a neighbor's family mentioned they'd encountered a group of elves while walking to town one night. Later, all they remembered was that time seemed long and stretched and that their memories were erased after coming in contact with the elves. Not one of them knew what had happened or how they got back home. It was very mysterious. Gram also attested to seeing leprechauns occasionally in the countryside of Ireland. They moved very fast, and she could never outrun them.

* * *

When my brother, Gustav, and I were teens, my parents were best friends with another couple, Babe and Ernie. They were like true family members to us, and we always looked forward to seeing them. They would light up a room when they entered. Gustav and I especially loved to hear Ernie tell us stories of his fun and lively experiences.

In order for Babe and Ernie to visit us, they had to drive on a road that cut through the pine barrens. Since they lived in Forked River, New Jersey, and we in Allentown, it was a one-hour trip, mostly through miles and miles of dense pine trees on each side of the road. One night when Ernie visited, he told about his last late-night drive home to Forked River. At approximately 2:45 a.m., while driving home, Babe was sleeping, but in his headlight beams, he noticed a group of very little beings along the side of the road. They were all gathered together and moving slowly.

As he approached them, he quickly tried to rouse Babe, but by the time he did, the group had quickly scurried into the woods. He explained they were very little and not quite human. He said he had made hundreds of trips through those very pines, as he commuted each day to work in Princeton, and he'd never seen anything like that before.

Gustav and I were especially fascinated by this story. I have heard that elves exist in a section of the Black Forest in Germany. Now, I don't discount that they live in New Jersey too.

We wish our good friends were still with us. Unfortunately, they were both killed in a car accident by a drunk driver on their way home from my parents' house before they even reached the pine lands.

*   *   *

My first encounter with the fairies was when I was a little girl. I found the world of Grimm's fairy tales. My world became magical with wishes and magical wands. As I was growing up, I received little fairies as gifts. Someone would just show up with a fairy and a message of hope, faith, and trust. I believed in the magic of the fairies, gnomes, angels, and unicorns.

As a child, I would always see small blue lights, especially when I was out in nature. I would see these tiny lights and would be filled with joy, knowing these tiny, beautiful imps were always around me.

When my godson was four years old, he started to call me his fairy godmother. Again, the fairies showed up in my life. To see the world through the eyes of a child is magic in itself. Being a "fairy godmother" is a very special honor. I since have become a fairy godmother to other children.

I truly believe the fairies are real. Just because we cannot see them does not mean they are not real. The fairies bring magic to our world. Their magic is in believing. We create with magic.

I honor the fairies and know without a doubt they are real. Anything is possible when you believe.

—Hilda P.

*   *   *

My dad passed away on February 2, 2007. He was picky with a lot of things, and one of them was that he did not like the color yellow. On the day he passed away, when we arrived home from the hospital, there was a yellow butterfly flying in my parents' yard. Several places we went, we would see this yellow butterfly. At the funeral, the butterfly was in the cemetery. One day there was even a yellow butterfly on the bumper of my parents' car, just stuck there. This yellow butterfly is around us often. At the time he passed away, my children were ages five, four, and three, but they know about the butterfly and know that Pop-Pop is always around when we see it.

—Jamie R.

*   *   *

My father died in January 2014. Pop-Pop was a man who dearly loved his family. Even during his fight against an aggressive form of cancer, he offered support and guidance, jokes to lift our spirits, and his special hugs to comfort us. He taught us how to live with love and dignity and how to die with the same.

Pop-Pop was very close to all of his grandchildren but especially close to the three youngest, who are my kids. He never missed a momentous event in their lives and was involved in many of the ordinary ones too. School concerts and plays, newly discovered talents, favorite books waiting to be read again, bike rides and baseball, swimming in the pool—all things the kids looked forward to doing because Pop would be there. So the loss of their beloved Pop-Pop was hard for them to understand and accept.

Later that year, soon after we returned home from our first family vacation without Pop, the kids and I were playing in the yard. My daughter noticed a large yellow-and-black butterfly hovering near us. She followed it to one of the butterfly bushes and called her brothers over to look at it. They smiled and laughed as the butterfly flew toward them on its way to the next flower. My youngest son said the butterfly made him feel as happy, as Pop-Pop always did. The date was September 4, 2014, which would have been my father's eightieth birthday.

In September 2015, my daughter was playing outside when she noticed a large yellow-and-black butterfly hovering near her, next to the butterfly bush. She took a photo of it, came into the house, and excitedly told everyone the Pop-Pop butterfly was back! I have to admit it looked remarkably like one we'd seen the year before. I took a photo of it too.

We didn't think about it again until the next summer. My kids wondered if Pop-Pop Butterfly, as it became known, would return that year. I wondered the same thing and secretly hoped it would. The answer came in September, when Pop-Pop Butterfly made a glorious return. We took photos of it, and each of the kids told it stories of what had happened in their lives since they saw it last. Pop-Pop Butterfly seemed to listen, moving to the next flower only when they were done speaking.

I don't know if it's the same butterfly that visits us every year, but it sure looks like it is. More important, it *feels* like it is. We're eagerly waiting for September to come again. The kids have so much to tell Pop-Pop Butterfly. This year, I do too.

—Matt S.

Wherever is love and loyalty, great purposes and lofty souls, even though in a hovel or a mine, there is fairyland.

—Charles Kingsley

REFERENCES

http://www.brainyquotes.com.

Devlin, Sadhbh. "A Guide to Finding Fairies: 15 Magical Places in Ireland." (2015).

http://www.wherewishescomefrom.com.

Fairchild, Mary. "What Does the Bible Say About Angels?" (2011). http://christianity.about.com/od/whatdoesthebiblesay/a/angelbible.htm.

http://www.fairygardening.com.

Goddidntsaythat.com. "God Didn't Say That Unicorns, Dragons, and Other Animals You Meet in the Bible." (2010). https://goddidntsaythat.com/2010/03/23/unicorns-dragons-and-other-animals-you-meet-in-the-bible/.

http://www.goodreads.com

Hag, Ming. "Survey: Tooth Fairy's 2016 Cash Payouts Hit All-Time High." (2017). https://www.usatoday.com.

Halloween. Directed by John Carpenter. Compass Internal Pictures, 1978.

Lock Haven University. "The Case of the Cottingley Fairies." (2018).

https://www.lockhaven.edu/~dsimanek/cooper.htm.

Luna's Grimoire. "Luna's Grimoire The Fae and Elementals: The Realm of Earth." (2012).

https://www.lunasgrimoire.com/grimoires.

Mom Junction. "100 Breathtaking, Fairy, Mermaid and Magical Baby Names." (2016).

http://www.momjunction.com/articles/magical-fairy-enchanting-mermaid-baby-names_00407880.

Pitz, Marylynne. "The Extensive Gardens of Winterthur Brim with Colors." (2014). http://Pitz/Pittsburg Post-Gazette.com.

http://www.quotesgarden.com.

Reilly, Jill. "Away with the fairies? University lecturer claims to have photographed real-life tiny tinkerbells flying through the air in the British countryside." (2015). http://www.dailymail.co.uk/news/article-2596119/Away-fairies-University-lecturer-claims-photographed-real-life-tiny-tinkerbells-flying-air-British-countryside.html.

Taylor, Melissa. "8 Reasons Why Fairy Tales Are Essential to Childhood." (2012). http://www.wyrmtalespress.com/wp-content/uploads/2015/05/Resources.pdf.

http://www.urbandictionary.com.

Wise, Lindsay. McClatchy DC Bureau. (2015). lwise@mcclatchydc.com.

Journal

Journal

Journal

Journal

Journal